Israel Without Zionism

ISRAEL WITHOUT ZIONISM

A Plan for Peace in the Middle East

by URI AVNERY

Collier Books, New York, New York

Collier-Macmillan Ltd., London

The Macmillan Company
866 Third Avenue, New York, N.Y. 10022
Collier-Macmillan Canada Ltd., Toronto, Ontario

Library of Congress Catalog Card Number: 71-165565

First Collier Books edition 1971

Israel Without Zionism was originally published in
hardcover by The Macmillan Company as *Israel
Without Zionists*.

Printed in the United States of America

Contents

Prologue

1: One Israeli

BEFORE I start this book, I want to say who I am and why I write it.

I don't pretend to be objective about Israel. I don't believe anyone is, or can be. There is something in the air of our country that leads to extremes. The light of summer is extreme. So are the rains of winter. The prophets were extreme people indeed, who did not believe in subtle hints. The Hebrew language itself is not given to understatement. Today nearly everything written about Israel is propaganda. Israel is either a holy place, full of upright pioneers, heroic warriors and virtuous maidens, or it is a den of robbers, cruel adventurers and shameless women, who have fallen upon an innocent people and raped a country.

I shall try, in this book, to present a different picture. I believe both sides are human, partly right and partly wrong. I want to show how two great historical movements, both authentic, both imbued with high ideals, clashed on the ancient battlefields of Palestine, vainly trying to destroy each other, succeeding only in twisting each other's souls.

Yet, while trying to do justice to both, I know that, belonging to one side, I shall not be objective. I am an Israeli. Like most of us, I am immensely proud of the achievements of my people in many fields. Like some of us, I am also acutely aware of our shortcomings and failures.

I am an Israeli who believes, passionately, in peace —but who has lived most of his life in war, and who is writing on the morrow of the latest and most dramatic battle among the Semitic nations, the 1967 so-called Six-Day War among Israel and the Arab countries— Egypt, Jordan and Syria.

One's ideas are the outcome of one's experiences. These experiences are, therefore, relevant. My personal story may help in understanding my ideas. I shall try to set it down—not because it is exceptional, but rather because it is typical.

*   *   *

My name is biblical, Uri, meaning light. Avner, or Abner, was the field marshal of King David, a figure I always liked. I was not born with this name. I gave it to myself. Like most of my age group in what was then Palestine, I changed my name immediately on reaching age eighteen. With this one act we declared our independence from our past; we broke with it irrevocably. The Jewish Diaspora, the world of our parents, their culture and their background—we wanted nothing more to do with. We were a new race, a new people, born the day we set foot on the soil of Palestine. We were Hebrews, rather than Jews; our new Hebrew names proclaimed this.

Actually, I was just ten years old when my parents brought me to Palestine. Even then, politics preoccupied me. I spent my first ten years in Germany. I was six when Hitler gained his first great victory at the polls. After that, the Nazi bid for power was the major influence in our lives. The endless parades of the brown-shirted storm troopers, the street battles between Nazis and Communists, the uniformed private armies of the many parties—these were the landscape of my early youth. Politics provided the main theme of conversation during family meals. Politics was the decisive factor—immensely more serious, more important, even, than the music of Brahms, which my father loved.

My father was a banker. Ours was a middle-class family, well-to-do, comfortable. Like his father before him, my father was imbued with the spirit of a German humanist education, steeped in Latin and ancient Greek, deeply rooted in an unassuming idealism which lasted all his life.

My father was also a Zionist. When he married my mother, in 1913, some of his friends gave him as a wedding gift a document stating that a tree had been planted in his name in Palestine. But Zionism, in pre-Hitler Germany, did not mean immigration to Palestine; I don't believe this idea ever entered my father's head. It meant, first of all, to be nonconformist (and I strongly suspect my father amused himself by upsetting the assimilationists around him, who hated Zionism). It also meant an awareness of the suffering of the Jews elsewhere, and a sympathy for the striving of the few pioneers who were trying to build a new country in the Near East—a place too far away to be quite real.

Yet Zionism saved our lives. I never forgot this when later I became a non-Zionist, perhaps an anti-Zionist.

I was nine years old when Hitler came to power. The brown terror broke loose the year I started high school. I found myself the only Jewish pupil there. As I remember it, every day or two some ancient victory of German arms was celebrated. All the pupils would be assembled in the great hall and made to sing the old and new patriotic songs. I remember one day—I believe it was the day of the battle of Belgrade—I stood small and alone among a thousand German boys who were singing the blood-churning hymn of Naziism, the *Horst Wessel* song. I did not sing, nor did I raise my hand in the Nazi salute like all the others. After it was finished, a group of my classmates told me that if I ever failed again to raise my arm while the hymn of the new Germany was being sung, they would "show me."

They never did. A week later we were gone from Germany for good.

I believe my father was one of the first German Jews to realize what was going on. He saw the handwriting on the wall the day the Nazis came to power. He was able to see it because his Zionist beliefs conditioned him to an awareness of the viciousness of anti-Semitism and to the utter hopelessness of combatting it.

So one day in January, 1933, my father went to the police department in Hanover to get his emigration permit. The police officers were astonished. "But Mr. Ostermann," they said, "you are a German like us. Your family has always lived in Germany. Nothing could happen to you here!"

Our relatives and friends were even more outspoken. Their worst suspicions about my father's peculiarities were confirmed. "You are completely crazy," they told him, "running away like this. Nothing can happen to us. This is a civilized country. This fellow Hitler is just making a lot of noise. He knows he can't exist without us. He'll evict some Polish Jews—and a good thing, too—but that will be all." We, the four children, heard and remembered.

But my father was a stubborn man. He knew he was right, even if he could not prove it. We sold everything and left.

The last days were hectic. Somehow we suspected that some of my father's business associates had denounced him to the Gestapo. So our family split, each parent taking two children, to cross the frontier as quietly as possible. For me, as a child, it was an exciting night. My mother kept losing things. Our train reached the French border, the Nazi officials checked our papers, a wave of the hand, and that was that. The train moved onward—into France. (Since then France has remained for me a symbol of freedom. I love France. I kept on loving it when I set up the Israeli Committee for Algerian Liberation and supported the Algerian *Front de Libération Nationale* [FLN] in its fight against the French.)

*   *   *

Some two weeks later we stood on the deck of a ship as the shores of Palestine slowly approached. For the children it was a new and exciting world. We knew about it from books, from the wonderful stories our instructors in the Zionist youth movement in Hanover had read to us.

But what did our parents feel at that moment? I have often wondered. What immense courage must have been theirs! Here was my father, having led an ordered life for 45 years, encumbered by a wife and four children, having to start a completely new life in a strange

country, struggling with the words of a strange language
(one he was never to learn).

It was a hard country, a different life. The little capital my father brought with him he quickly lost in various endeavors. He did not want to invest the money in
real estate in the new country. He did not want to have
anything to do with commerce, banking, and specula-
tion. By the end of our first year, our position was
desperate. As a last resort, my father and mother set up
a laundry delivery business, both of them working
twelve hours a day. This they did for eighteen years
until my father died, more or less from overwork.

Long before that he had learned that all our friends
and relatives, those who had mocked us when we left,
perished during the awful years the Jews call The Holocaust. Later, when I covered the Eichmann trial as a
journalist, my thoughts went back to my father, whose
intuition had saved our lives. I am deeply grateful to
him. I remember him carrying the laundry on his bi-
cycle, dead tired but irrepressibly cheerful, happy as he
had never been behind an executive desk in Hanover.
He was a real human being.

*   *   *

As a boy in Palestine, I was sent off for a few months
to learn Hebrew in Nahalal, the legendary settlement in
the valley of Ezreel. After I rejoined my parents in Tel
Aviv, I went to elementary school until I was thirteen. I
never went back to school after that. With my parents
working so hard and the depression steadily getting
worse in Palestine, I did not want to go on to high
school. I wanted to earn a living, and formal schooling
bored me. I was always getting ahead of my class; the

school system seemed a wastefully slow way of acquiring knowledge.

After a highly unsuccessful try at mechanics, I went to work as a lawyer's clerk. Here I began to see life as it really was: the poverty of the many; the difference between the Arabs of Jaffa, where some of the courts were located, and the Jews of neighboring Tel Aviv; the supercilious superiority of our British masters who ran the courts and the police.

One day at court, another lawyer's clerk asked me what I thought about the political situation. I said I thought our leaders were disgraceful.

"What are you going to do about it?" he asked. I told him I did not know.

"Well, some of us think we know," he said. "There is an organization. . . ."

Thus I heard, for the first time, the name of the *Irgun* —the National Military Organization, which became from that moment the center of my life.

Arab terrorism was raging in the country at the time. Jews were being ambushed and killed every few days. The British seemed to be incapable of putting a stop to these acts, and the Jews, ever suspicious of British perfidy, believed that the British were secretly supporting the Arabs. Much later I realized that these "disturbances," as we called them in Hebrew, were in fact an Arab rebellion, a last desperate, and wholly inefficient, try of the Palestinian Arab nation to get rid of the British overlords and the Jewish immigrants, who looked to them like a rabble of foreigners trying to take over their country. But at the time I saw only that our people were being killed, that the hypocritical British were doing nothing to stop them, and it looked to me as if our established leaders, preaching *havlaga*, or self-restraint, were acting like cowards.

There was only one way a boy could respond to the situation. We had to kill Arabs in return, kick out the British, and turn our own official leaders, the people of the Jewish Agency, out of office. When the British hanged Shlomo Ben-Yossef, a young *Irgun* member who had thrown a bomb at an Arab bus after a similar Arab outrage, I knew what I had to do. The place of every self-respecting, upright young Hebrew was in the *Irgun*.

*   *   *

One day in the late summer of 1938, just before I turned fifteen, I got a message to appear at nine that night at a certain school building in a remote corner of old Tel Aviv. The password was "Samson and Delilah."

With pounding heart, I approached the building. It looked dark and menacing. No light showed. It seemed completely deserted. As soon as I entered, dark figures surrounded me. I stuttered the magic words, and they waved me on. This happened several times, until I was shunted into a room where a brilliant spotlight blinded me.

I nearly flunked the interview. When asked whether I hated the Arabs, I gave the wrong answer. I said no, I could fight the British without hating the Arabs. These seemed doubtful sentiments coming from a boy of fourteen. Yet somebody behind the light must have decided that I would still make a good underground soldier, for I was accepted.

The next year and a half were pure bliss. My life was circumscribed by a certainty I never knew again: We were doing the right thing. Our leaders, whom we did not know, were wise, heroic supermen. The Arabs and the British were the enemy, the Jewish Agency leaders were despicable ghetto Jews, we were the "Chosen Few" who would bring salvation to our people by acts of self-sacrifice.

We exercised. We marched. We toughened ourselves. We sang battle songs whose words described the great deeds of our ancient heroes, and our own creed: "In blood and fire did Judea fall, in blood and fire will Judea rise again." We learned to use pistols, draw quickly, shoot from the hip—of course without ammunition because a live bullet was as precious as gold. When I was entrusted with the company stock of three pistols to hide in my bed, I was overjoyed.

Our families were forgotten. Work was a nuisance, to be dispatched as quickly as possible. Life was dismantling a parabellum and putting it together again blindfolded (I think I can still do it). Sex was standing with an *Irgun* girl in a dark street corner, pretending to be lovers, one hand on a hidden button ready to warn our comrades training on the roof of the approach of police.

We distributed leaflets describing the glorious deeds of our older comrades—who had planted a bomb in a crowded Arab market, or killed a police officer who had tortured a boy found in the possession of arms. We demonstrated against the British, burning the government offices when the British published, in May, 1939, the White Paper that put an end to Jewish immigration, thereby blocking the last avenue of escape for Jews who still could get out of Nazi Germany.

It was a great life. Arrest and torture were always just around the corner, but we lived every minute, knowing we were right. Life had meaning, purpose. When I close my eyes, I can still see a hundred and twenty boys and girls at attention in a blacked-out cellar, standing behind their trusted officers (clerks and salesmen in civilian life), singing—softly, so that no sound would escape the room—the hymn of the *Irgun*:

> Unknown soldiers are we, without uniforms,
> Around us but darkness and death,
> We have joined the army for life,
> Only death will relieve us from the ranks . . .

* * *

And then, quite suddenly, our world came crashing down around us. The *Irgun* split wide open.

Beginning with a clash of personalities, the split soon became a clash of principles and degenerated quickly into an orgy of mutual abuse, such as only a fight within a family or a sect can produce. The unknown leaders suddenly assumed names—Raziel, Stern—and accused each other of being Fascists, British agents, traitors, spies for the police. Our secure little world was disintegrating. Commanders, as lost as their men, wandered between the warring factions. Our company commander, an architect, whom we admired and imitated, joined Stern, the extremist leader who believed that we should make common cause even with the Nazis and Fascists in order to overthrow British imperialism.

One fateful night, we were assembled in a dark schoolroom to hear a speech by one of the Sternists. We did not see him. A powerful voice came out of the darkness, starting off with the words: "We follow our leaders into battle—as long as they lead us into battle."

The other side, he told us, was prepared to stop the fight against the British for the duration of World War II. We, the fighters, would carry on. England was weak. This was the time to strike.

At the end of the speech, he said: "But if there are any among us who do not have the strength and the courage to carry on, let them stand now and leave." The assumption, obviously, was that no one would dare to.

I stood up and left. Walking the streets for hours, I felt alone and forsaken, all certainty dissolved. But the desperation slowly lifted, new ideas—half felt but suppressed until that moment—rushed in. I was only fifteen, but I think it was the night I grew up.

Two things became clear to me before the night was over. I knew that I would devote my life to politics, that compared to politics everything else was unimportant, wasteful. I was going to teach myself the things one must know to be effective in politics—history, military science, psychology, economics, social affairs. I also knew that I did not agree with the *Irgun* on many points. I did not agree with its reactionary stand, its anti-socialism, its contempt for the *kibbutzim* and the workers' movement. I did not agree with the concept of the Chosen Few. Few there may be at the beginning of any movement, but the job of the few is to influence, to educate, to win over the many.

* * *

The next few years, while the *Irgun* broke up, reformed and resumed the attack, and the Stern group set the tempo of armed struggle against the British, I tried to formulate these rough ideas into a system. After much trial and error, I succeeded in forming a small political group. It created an uproar which lasted until the 1948 Israeli-Arab war.

We called ourselves the Young Palestinians. But because our publication, which appeared irregularly whenever we made enough money, was called the *Bama'avak*, meaning Struggle, we were generally called the *Bama'avak* group. Our message was quite simple and quite heretical: In Palestine a new Hebrew nation is born. This nation belongs to the Middle East. While throwing off the British yoke, it must help the other nations in this part of the world to throw out their imperialist masters. Our national movement, together with the Arab national movement, must form an integrated, coordinated Semitic front. A unified Semitic Region (for which we invented a new Hebrew word, *Ha-Merkhav Ha-Shemi*, which became our trademark) must become the common aim of all our struggles. The struggles themselves must become a unifying process, melting all our differences into one great movement toward national liberation, social reform, and planned regional progress.

We were accused of many things—of trying to cut ourselves off from the Jewish people throughout the world, of forsaking Western culture, of burying Zionism, of giving aid and comfort to the Arab enemy. But the public debate that we loosed carried these ideas into many quarters. We felt that we were the wave of the future, the authentic new voice of Hebrew youth.

In the fall of 1947, I wrote a booklet called "War and Peace in the Semitic Region," warning against partition and trying to formulate a practical alternative. We translated the summary of the argument into

Arabic and sent it to every newspaper and political group throughout the Middle East.

But it was too late. A few days afterward, the war which we call in Hebrew the War of Liberation broke out.

When the radio announced that the plan for the partition of Palestine into a Jewish state and an Arab state was approved by a majority of the United Nations General Assembly, the masses poured into the streets dancing with joy. The age-old dream, so it seemed, had been realized. Jews had found a national home at long last, free and independent, where they could live at peace.

That fateful night, my few friends and I worked feverishly to publish the last issue of *Bama'avak*. We warned that partition would not bring peace, that a great war was imminent, that the historical clash between the Hebrew and Arab nations would go on in a different form until Semitic unity is achieved.

On the first page, there appeared a poem which I recall often these past few months:

> We swear to you, our motherland,
> On this day of your dismemberment:
> Great and united you will arise again.
> We, your sons, Hebrew and Arab,
> Will carry your wound in our hearts,
> Until the day comes that sees you again
> One country, from the sea to the desert.

* * *

That night the war with the Arabs broke out, and we saw before us the choice which we were to face again and again. Should or should we not fight in this war we

thought was a historical tragedy and which, we believed, could have been avoided if wiser council had
prevailed on both sides? Losing the war meant physical
annihilation of our people, the end of our nation. Shirk-
ing our duty, for whatever reason, would render us in-
effective after the dust of war had settled. In the hour of
Israel's danger, our place was in the combat units,
peace our unrelinquished goal.

I joined the *Giv'ati* brigade, a *Haganah* formation
charged with defending the South of Israel. After several months as a private in the infantry, fighting for the
road to Jerusalem and later against the Egyptian army
moving up from Gaza, I took part in creating a new
type of combat unit, a commando team mounted on
open jeeps, which took the place of light tank cavalry,
making up with speed and fire-power for the lack of
any protective armor.

In June an Egyptian unit cut off a *kibbutz* called
Negba, a focal point of our defense. We were ordered
to drive the enemy out of their fortified position on Hill
105. In pitch darkness, in eight open jeeps—each
equipped with two machine-guns blazing away—we
literally overran the open trenches. Next day we were
told we had won the decisive engagement of the war, in
appreciation of which we received the honorary title of
Samson's Foxes. ("So Samson went and caught three
hundred foxes, and took torches, and he turned them
tail to tail, and put a torch between each pair of tails.
And when he had set fire to the torches, he let the foxes
go into the standing grain of the Philistines. . . .")

Much later I read than an Egyptian officer named
Gamal Abd-el-Nasser was wounded in that battle. We
must have been very close to each other in the melee.
This curious association between Nasser and the Foxes

continued throughout the war. We must have met—without being properly introduced—dozens of times in the darkness of night battles.

Eventually, on the last day of our brigade on the Southern Front, I was wounded in a sector near Faluga commanded by Nasser. By that time, I was a platoon leader. My men were a strange mixture of Moroccan, Tripolitanian and Turkish Jewish volunteers, who had come to us straight off the ships. I had trained them myself, using gestures and simple words; we could hardly converse. That day, I was told to relieve another platoon, on a little hill opposite the Egyptian position, in broad daylight. I knew the order was quite wrong, but after twelve months of battle, one did not really care very much any more. I went up to the hill, left my men on the reverse slope and met the other platoon leader on the top. Standing there casually, reviewing the enemy position, we came suddenly under murderous machine-gun fire. Some bullets hit me in the abdomen and the arm. It was always a wonder to me how my men, those green recruits, rushed up and got me out of that death-trap, under fire. Because I owe them my life, I am easily angered by loose talk about the inferiority of Oriental immigrants—a familiar attitude of mind in Israeli conversation.

* * *

All through the war, I became increasingly upset over many features of the new state, which assumed its form somewhere behind the backs of the young people who manned the fighting brigades. I did not like the identification of the state with religion, the spoils system practiced among the functionaries of the old party machines, the dependence on foreign aid, the social set-up itself. But most of all I objected to the sterility of the new state's approach to the main problem: how to achieve peace with the Arabs. The war turned combat soldiers, those of us who survived, into passionate partisans of peace.

Communicating these feelings in endless conversations in the field, around campfires and between cactus hedges, I found that many were shared by my comrades. We decided to do something about them, in one form or another, after the war. The opportunity came quite soon. After I came out of the hospital, while waiting for my friends to finish their military service, I published my war diary in book form under the title, *In the Fields of the Philistines*. Unexpectedly, it became a bestseller. The proceeds, together with some money we scraped together, allowed us to buy a moribund, innocuous little weekly paper, *Ha'olam Hazeh* ("This World").

Since Passover 1950, *Ha'olam Hazeh*, also nicknamed "A Certain Weekly" because its many enemies in official circles refuse to mention its name, has become an Israeli institution as unique as a *kibbutz*. Its journalistic formula is a mixture of extremes—*Foreign Affairs Quarterly* and *Playboy*, Walter Lippmann and Louella Parsons, *Time* and *Ramparts*. It is a mass-circulation magazine, but people say it preaches heresy; it is boycotted by the army, but popular with army officers; detested by the government, yet indispensable to anyone in government who wants to know what's going on, especially in government. Leading the fight for separation of state and synagogue, against corruption, for civil rights and a written constitution (still missing), for equal rights to the Arab minority and many other issues, it continues to be mainly identified in the public mind with the fight for Israeli-Arab peace.

The turbulent history of *Ha'olam Hazeh* reads like a cheap thriller. There have been three bomb attacks on its offices, during which several people were wounded; one night attack on its editors, in which my hands were broken; an officially inspired economic boycott, which still lasts after many years, cutting deep into its advertising; several trials at criminal prosecution for sedition (all squashed by the courts).

During the 1956 Sinai war, to which we strongly objected, the editors of *Ha'olam Hazeh*, together with some like-minded public figures, formed an ideological group, which we called Semitic Action. After year-long deliberations, this group published the Hebrew Manifesto, a program of 126 points, including the establishment of a federation in Palestine and a great Semitic confederacy throughout the Middle East, the return of the refugees, and many other ideas we had been fighting for since 1950 in the "Certain Weekly." Semitic Action never became a political factor, but its voice was loud and clear.

The creation of a real political force came about in 1965, as a culmination of the battle of *Ha'olam Hazeh* itself. The Eshkol government, under pressure from the religious parties, promulgated a special law aimed at curbing the publication's outspoken style. This happened on the eve of elections, and pushed me into parliamentary politics. Encouraged by the public outcry against such a blatant move to silence the magazine's voice, we set up our own list for the 1965 elections. After a hectic campaign, we received 1.2 per cent of the national vote, enough to put me into Israel's parlia-

ment, the *Knesset*, as a one-man parliamentary group.*
Significantly and paradoxically, in three sectors of the
population we received a much higher percentage of the
vote: in the army, among the Arabs who live in Israel,
and in several border settlements. The young and the
vigorous wanted a new force, and they gave us the
opportunity.

For the two years leading up to the June war, I
voiced in parliament the ideas propounded in *Ha'olam
Hazeh*, the ideas which are the outgrowth of the experiences of my generation and which I shall try now to
define.

* In the 1968 elections the *Ha'olam Hazeh* party won two
seats.

2: The War Nobody Wanted

I was still in bed, after a long night's work, when the sirens sounded.

For the first second or two I didn't recognize the sound. It surprised me. Then I said, "Well. So it has started." I hadn't expected the war, which I knew was coming, to start just that day.

My wife wanted us to go down to the air raid shelter. She was very proud of the shelter, because, as a member of the House Committee, she had been entrusted, a few days before, with preparing the shelter for war. Until that time, the shelter was considered a joke and was used by everyone as a store room for things we didn't know what to do with. Now it was clean, empty, provided with water and buckets of sand.

I did not want to go down. Even during the 1948 war, I always preferred open trenches to closed shelters. What's more, a high-ranking officer of the Air Force had promised me a few days previously that in case of war not a single enemy plane would reach Tel

Aviv. In Israel you believe the promises of the armed forces; they are the only promises you do believe.

I was in bed in Tel Aviv instead of out in a trench somewhere among the sand dunes of the Negev, because as a member of Parliament I am exempt from military service. I believe that very few men of my age group, however, were still in Tel Aviv on June 5, 1967. As a matter of fact, Parliament was reconvening that very day, and I had to go up to Jerusalem for the session. After listening to some dramatic but newsless radio reports about the advance on Sinai, I drove to Jerusalem, fifty miles away.

I was the only civilian on the road. My white Mustang contrasted curiously with the immense number of tanks and half-tracks making their way toward Jerusalem. The Jordanians had started to shell Israeli territory, and the number of troops rolling eastward confirmed my guess that we would mount an attack on the Jordanian front. A foreign observer would have found the scene on the road chaotic. Tanks and half-tracks, command cars, jeeps, and guns were moving, overtaking each other, with military police here and there trying to create some order. But it was all going on in a thoroughly Israeli style. Our army is composed of people who know exactly what their job is and don't need any outward show of rigid order and discipline to do it.

What struck me was the excited, nearly gay, mood of everybody. It was an atmosphere of immense relief, after twenty-one days of mounting tension and uncertainty. Whatever doubts may have formed during those three weeks of worry seemed to have evaporated once the armor hit the road. The soldiers in the half-tracks were grinning, shouting jocular curses and making the "V" sign at the people in the tanks, who would answer in kind. One of the young tank commanders, recognizing me, raised three fingers instead of two. Three fingers signified the first letter of the Hebrew word *shalom*, meaning peace, which was a symbol I had adopted during my election campaign. There was something curiously appropriate in this gesture of a young soldier, going up to what must have been his first battle, making the sign of peace. Yet everybody thought that day that we were at war again to achieve peace.

Reaching the *Knesset*, after many detours, I found the new, imposing but rather ugly building under heavy bombardment—the only parliament in the world, it occurred to me, within one mile of enemy artillery. Shells were falling near, and after a short session in which we approved some bills to finance the war, we were shooed into the air raid shelter. It was there that a friend of mine, a confidant of the Prime Minister, whispered to me the news that the enemy air force had already been virtually annihilated. This meant that the war had been won before it really started. It changed our mood from one of deepest worry to one of exhilaration. The prospect of a long war with thousands and thousands of casualties was replaced by the prospect of lightning victory.

I am not going to tell the story of this war. Some books have already been written about it, and many more will be. But I would like to trace briefly the events which led up to it—not to reveal new facts, but rather to show how this war happened, like an event in a Greek tragedy, without anybody wanting it, with everybody behaving like actors playing parts written by a hidden playwright, saying words written by somebody else, all according to an inner logic which no one quite understood.

This logic was the result of events going back seventy years and more. They were inherent in everything that happened that month. They—the events, the reasons, the attitudes resulting from them, the whole vicious circle of which this war was just one element—are the subject of this book.

* * *

May 15 was a beautiful day, sunny and hot. It was Independence Day, the most festive day of the year, when the birth of the State of Israel in the middle of the war is commemorated by a military parade. This year the parade was held in Jerusalem, and was therefore quite small. According to the Armistice Agreement, neither Israel nor Jordan was allowed to bring armor, artillery or military aircraft into the Jerusalem area, and our government more or less complied with these restrictions. The parade was limited to infantry units. Yet 200,000 Israelis, one out of every twelve in the whole country, showed up to applaud the army, which plays such a big part in our nation's life.

There was no reason for anxiety that day. The state seemed more secure than ever, war seemed far off. Certainly there had been trouble brewing all through the last few months on the Syrian frontier, with armed infiltrators planting bombs in border settlements, and various *kibbutzim* shelled from time to time. Something, everyone felt, would have to be done about it sooner or later, perhaps quite soon; a full-scale attack by our army on the fortified positions on the Syrian hills seemed imminent. But we knew that the Syrian Army was a negligible force, and such an attack would not rank as war by Israeli standards. We knew that war could come only if Egypt wanted it. And Egypt was busy with a small war in Yemen.

Nothing could have been further off than the idea of war on that sunny day; we lolled around on the Tel Aviv seashore, waiting for the festivities to start, as we listened to the transistor radio blaring old marching songs, including one I had written myself about Samson's Foxes. Yet at that very minute General Yitzhak Rabin, the Chief of Staff, approached Prime Minister Levi Eshkol on the reviewing stand in Jerusalem and whispered something in his ear. A most urgent message had just come through. As gay and unconcerned as everyone else's until that moment, Eshkol's face suddenly clouded over. The next day we read it in the newspaper: the headline was devoted to the parade, but underneath was a second important item, announcing that the Egyptian President, Gamal Abd-el-Nasser, had ordered his troops into the Sinai Peninsula, opposite our southern frontier.

It will always remain a mystery what exactly were Nasser's motives. The most plausible explanation is that he had reached the conclusion Israel was going to attack Syria as a part of a devious American plan to overthrow a left-wing, pro-Soviet regime in Damascus. He could not stand by idly while this happened, because this would have shattered forever his claim as the leader and defender of the Arab world. His fortunes at low ebb, the Egyptian President must have believed that doing something dramatic yet costless would be an easy way to retrieve them.

Nasser's assumptions were partly right and partly wrong. Israel was very close to attacking Syria, as our

Prime Minister openly declared on the eve of Independence Day; but this had absolutely nothing to do with any American plan, nor with the social ideology of the Syrian dictatorship. The sole motivation was to put an end to acts of sabotage perpetrated in Israel by terrorists which, everyone in Israel believed, were organized by the Syrians.

Now the conscious and unconscious beliefs and convictions of both sides, formed by the events of the last three generations, started to exert their profound influence and lead to yet another war. Nasser, like all Arabs, implicitly believes that Israel is the creation of Western imperialism, and therefore acts automatically according to Western interests; as it was clearly in the American interest to get rid of the Syrian regime, it was quite obvious in the Arab mind that an Israeli threat to Syria must be a part of an American plan.

Nasser just couldn't understand that Israel's sole concern, at the moment, was to put a stop to terrorist acts—and he made his first big mistake. If he had concentrated his troops in Sinai, and at the same time had demanded that the Syrian and the Arab Palestinian terrorist organizations put a stop to the guerrilla warfare, this would have been welcomed in Israel. It would have confirmed the general picture of Nasser, for the time being at least, as a moderate leader who did not want war. Yet Nasser did not do this. He declared that his troops would attack Israel if the Israeli Army attacked Syria—without making any suggestion for ending the problem which made such an attack on Syria necessary in Israeli eyes. He seemed to be telling us: "The terrorists will invade Israel in ever-increasing numbers, making life in Israel increasingly intolerable. But if you react, we shall destroy you." This is how it sounded in

Israel. The psychological abyss between the two nations is so immense that Nasser did not, and could not, realize this in time.

Nor did Nasser understand the automatic reaction of the Israeli the minute he realized that a powerful military force was being concentrated on Israel's frontier. Our country is small, much smaller than most people realize. Our security is based, first of all, on our ability, by the prestige of our army, to deter any enemy from threatening our existence, and secondly, if this deterrent fails, to hit first and win quickly, thereby avoiding an invasion of our constricted territory. When Nasser marched his troops through Cairo, drums rolling and trumpets blaring, letting them pass beneath the windows of the American Embassy—instead of moving them quietly to the front—he hoped to intimidate Israel and dissuade her from taking military action; in actuality, he achieved the exact opposite. By posing the threat to our frontier, he rang the bell hidden in the unconscious mind of every Israeli, a signal which turns Israel, within the minute, from a peaceful country into an armed camp. It is the psychology of a besieged fortress. Let the sentry on the tower sound the alarm if an enemy force approaches, and everybody inside rushes to man the bastions.

*   *   *

Before Nasser realized that without really intending to, he had created a war-like situation overnight, he made a second mistake. Since the Sinai War in 1956, the frontiers between Israel and Egypt, as well as the shores of the controversial Gulf of Akaba had been patrolled by the United Nations Emergency Force. UNEF was not really a military factor, but rather a device enabling Nasser, without losing face in the Arab world, to avoid having to do anything which might provoke an Israeli attack. Most Arabs consider Israel an alien state, created by force in a country rightly belonging to the Arabs. For an Arab, therefore, it is quite unthinkable that the Egyptians, having gained control of the approaches to the Gulf of Akaba, on which the Israeli port of Elat is located, would let Israeli ships pass through. He would also have only contempt for an Arab government that would stop Arab terrorists from slipping through its frontier to spread violence in "occupied Palestine." But Nasser had known since 1956 that each of these acts would compel any Israeli government to mount a military attack. The presence of U.N. forces in these sensitive areas since 1956 allowed Nasser to leave the Straits open and his frontier closed without seeming to do so. Now, suddenly, Nasser changed the situation. His commander in the field asked the U.N. commander to remove his troops.

This event is still shrouded in mystery. What actually happened may have been one of the several misunderstandings of this pre-war phase which seemed quite irrational, yet were really logical results of the attitudes prevailing in the Middle East. Nasser, so it seems, did not really want the U.N. forces to leave; he just wanted some of them to shift a little. This would make his move to the frontier appear more threatening, strike joy in the hearts of the Arabs and intimidate Israel. But the U.N. commander could not move his troops without the consent of U.N. Secretary General U Thant. U Thant decided that if he had to move part of his troops, he would destroy the effectiveness of the whole force; suddenly Nasser had to choose between reversing him-

self, which would make him look ridiculous, and ordering all the U.N. troops to leave—which is what he
did.

The act of removing the U.N. troops dramatized the
situation in Israeli eyes. Until then no one took the
Egyptian move quite seriously. The idea that Nasser
was busy in the Yemen and unable to risk a war with
Israel was still deeply rooted. Overnight, this belief disappeared. The Israeli Army had to prepare for an Arab
attack.

You have to understand the Israeli Army in order to
realize what this meant. Nasser, commanding a regular
army, could move his divisons here or there without
changing the texture of life in Egypt. But Israel has
only a very small regular army. Its wartime army con-
sists mainly of reserves, a full mobilization of almost
the entire population. Once the reserves are called up,
the economy grinds to a halt. The men of Israel literally
disappear from the streets, the offices, the factories, the
coffee shops. The whole country changes, visually and
materially. By compelling the Israeli Army to mobilize,
Nasser had brought the Middle East to the brink of war
without quite realizing it. He still, so I believe, wanted
to avoid war, not out of an innate love for peace, but
because he was aware that he could not win in any
direct military confrontation with Israel.

But now something much worse occurred. The third
great mistake was about to be committed. When U
Thant ordered his troops out, in unseemly and undip-
lomatic haste, the Straits of Tiran were left unmanned.
Nasser had to fill the gap by putting his troops there,
whether he wanted to or not. And once they were there,
the awful question posed itself: Now that Egyptian

troops commanded the Straits again, how could they possibly permit ships of the hated Zionist enemy to pass through them to the port of Elat?

Logic would have dictated closing the eyes and pretending the Israeli ships didn't exist. Anyone could have guessed that renewing the blockade of the Straits would compel the Israeli government to open them by force; otherwise, the credibility of the Israeli military deterrent would be shattered—quite apart from the economic consequences of the blockade. The Israeli told himself, logically: We have said many times that we shall not tolerate such a blockade. If we back down now, every single Arab will believe that our military force is a bluff. If this belief spreads, there is nothing to hold back the Arabs from starting a guerrilla war along all our frontiers, cutting off the Jordan waters, and doing anything else they like. So we'd better fight now. Yet Nasser, who must have vaguely felt all this, could not back down either. Keeping the Straits open, now that the U.N. forces had disappeared, would have looked like downright cowardice. It would have lent credence to the argument of his enemies in the Arab world, who shrilly proclaimed him to be a secret collaborator of the Zionists. Nasser had to walk into the trap he had set for himself. On May 22, he announced that the Straits of Tiran would be closed to Israeli shipping.

I clearly recall the effect this had. We were having lunch at parliament when the radio announced the news. We were in the middle of a great debate on the situation. At the beginning of the debate some of us still voiced the fervent hope that peace could be preserved. After the radio announcement we all knew that war had become unavoidable.

A curious little incident throws light on the whole situation. The Egyptians declared at the same time that mines had been laid in the actual strait itself, a narrow passage between the Egyptian mainland and the little island of Tiran at the entrance of the Gulf of Akaba. Later, during the war, it was discovered the claim was entirely untrue: Not one single mine had in fact been laid. This being so, why did the Egyptians make such a claim, aggravating an already explosive situation? I later found out the reason, which now appears completely ridiculous, but which somehow symbolizes the dimension of misunderstanding. The Egyptians thought that by such a pronouncement they would for the time being deter Israeli ships from trying to force a passage, and relieve themselves of the necessity of shooting at the ships; thus the Egyptians hoped to avert the war. The result was, of course, the exact opposite. The idea of mines in the Straits made the whole situation look somehow irreversible in Israeli eyes.

* * *

People trying to analyze the events from the outside tend to forget one element. Yet this above all fanned the flames of war. In the Middle East, propaganda plays a decisive role. Millions of people all over the Arab world who can't read newspapers, and who wouldn't read them if they could, listen for hours on end to the radio, smoking their *narghila* and sipping their strong coffee in innumerable village coffee houses.

Israelis believe propaganda, certainly their own, but also that of the Arabs, especially if it confirms what they suspect anyhow, that the Arabs are out to kill them. For the Arabs, however, propaganda means something quite different. They love it, they adore it, and they certainly don't expect it to be an accurate presentation of facts. The Arab language is a very rich and beautiful one, and Arabs love it as Italians love music and the French love food. Words, beautiful words coming out of the radio, are for most Arabs intoxicating, making them forget a reality which is still far from satisfying their aspirations. Words easily become a substitute for reality.

It was, therefore, quite natural for Radio Cairo, transmitting in Arabic to the Arab world and in Hebrew to Israel, to utter the most blood-curdling threats and prophecies from the very beginning of the crisis. Turning on his radio, the Israeli heard that the hour of revenge had struck, that the Zionist robbers were going to be thrown into the sea, that Palestine would be liberated, that the refugees were about to return as a victorious army and take possession of their land again. Newspapers carried photographs of Nasser and his military chief, Abd-el-Hakim Amer, laughing outrageously while inspecting an Arab air force unit in Sinai. It looked sinister indeed. Merely irritating in another situation, but accompanied now by news reports of a thousand tanks massing along the frontier, the closing of the Straits, and the retreat of the U.N. forces, this propaganda was taken as a statement of intent, the declaration of actual Arab policy about to be set in motion.

The propaganda buildup seems to have been intended to impress the Israelis with the great superiority and confidence of the Arab army, in order to deter Israel from attack and leave Nasser in possession of a bloodless victory. The result was, again, the exact opposite. By now the Israelis knew they had to make war, and the great massed army in the barren wastes of the

Negev waited with growing impatience and irritability for the order. One cannot keep a citizens' army waiting for long without grave psychological and economic risks. Time, which was long for the Arabs, was very short for the Israelis. The decision could not be postponed much longer.

* * *

Yet on May 28, when the Israeli Government—by now in continuous session—was faced with the decision, it hesitated. Foreign Minister Abba Eban, who had just returned after trying to convince the Americans, the British and the French to run the blockade and force the issue, urged restraint. But restraint was unpopular. Nobody in Israel believes that foreigners will help us to survive. It is a deep Jewish belief, the outcome of many generations of persecutions and most especially of the experiences during the Nazi time, that no gentile would lift a finger to save Jewish lives. Unconsciously held by almost everyone in Israel, this attitude has a profound influence on public opinion and helps to explain still another paradox of the Middle East crisis. Nasser believed that Israel was an American puppet, and he hoped that by some deal with America he could keep the Israelis inactive. The Israelis, for their part, would not dream of putting their trust in America, or anyone else, in a crisis where their survival seemed at stake. But on May 28, opinion in the government—representing at the time a coalition of parties holding 75 out of 120 seats in the *Knesset* —was evenly split. Nine Ministers, including Levi Eshkol, voted for war. Nine other Ministers voted against it. The result was a tie, which meant that the decision was no.

But an unforeseen development had a devastating effect. Eshkol was to broadcast to the nation a keep-up-the-morale speech. There was still some time left to put the broadcast on tape, and the broadcasting experts, knowing his style, urged him to do so. Eshkol, an interesting personality in many ways, is a highly ineffectual speaker given to meandering sentences and long digressions which tend to peter out. Yet the Prime Minister, used to speaking in parliament, is confident of his ability to get his message through; he was going to read a prepared statement. Up to the last minute of the actual live broadcast, phrases were edited and re-edited. One adviser thought that a phrase about the need to have the forces retreat from the frontiers was psychologically unsound. You don't mention retreat in such a situation. So he put in the words "move the forces" instead. Unfortunately, he forgot to cross out the word "retreat." When Eshkol came on the air reading the statement in a tired voice, he started to hesitate and stammer when he reached this passage, trying to make out the wording and whispering with his advisers. All the people, the tense soldiers listening in the trenches, were suddenly struck with the idea that our supreme leader in this fateful hour was an old, tired, hesitating, stuttering party functionary. The reaction was an instinctive, unanimous demand for strong leadership.

The next four days, in Israel, were taken up by maneuvering to satisfy this demand. As a result, subtle changes in the situation went unheeded. On the same day that Eshkol made his by-now-famous speech, Nasser held a press conference in Cairo. Desperately frightened of the coming war, he looked for some way to extricate himself from the trap into which he had blundered. He talked of reactivating the Israeli-Egyp-

tian Armistice Commission, an institution held in great
contempt in Israel. He proposed to open discussions—
not with Israel, whose existence he does not recognize,
but with the world powers—concerning the whole
Palestinian problem. He had already told the Americans he was prepared to let all ships, even those carrying oil, pass through the Straits to Elat, as long as none
carried the Israeli flag.

In Cairo, these may have looked like far-reaching
efforts to relieve the crisis, going as far as they could
without looking like a retreat. In Jerusalem they did not
arouse the slightest notice. They all seemed irrelevant,
compared with one remark Nasser had made rather
casually, unaware that he had dropped a bombshell; to
Arab ears, after all, it was quite routine, even moderate. Nasser said in his press conference that if Israel
attacked either Syria or Egypt, this would lead to a war
in which the aim of the Arabs would be the final destruction of the State of Israel. In the atmosphere prevailing by this time, after hundreds of similar and more
extreme threats from Radio Cairo, it is no wonder that
the first part of the phrase was overlooked, or that it
seemed an irrelevant decoration. What came through
was a direct threat to destroy the State of Israel, the
annihilation of every single man, woman and child.

Two days later, while Israel was still busy reshuffling
its government, Nasser made his final miscalculation.
Looking for the best way to avoid an Israeli attack, he
had King Hussein of Jordan come to Cairo. This was
meant to say to the Israelis that if war started, it would
be waged all along Israel's extensive and indefensible
frontiers. The effect was electrifying. If there was any
hesitation left in Israel, it disappeared immediately.
The Egyptian-Jordanian military pact raised a spectre

dreaded by every Israeli: the possibility of a big Arab army, including Egyptians and Iraqis, attacking not from the relatively distant southern frontier, but also from the much closer and more exposed Jordanian border. (I can see the Jordanian frontier easily with the naked eye from the window of my apartment on the seashore of Tel Aviv. It is within easy artillery range.) The news that King Hussein had allied himself with his arch-enemy Nasser, putting his army under Egyptian command and agreeing to allow other Arab armies to join his on the Israeli front, meant only one thing to the Israelis: that they must hit immediately and destroy the Egyptian army before anyone had time to move into Jordan.

The next day, under immense public pressure, General Moshe Dayan was brought into the government and appointed Minister of Defense. The government was enlarged to include all major parties. Only 12 out of 120 members of the *Knesset*, including myself, were left out of the government coalition. Bringing in Dayan, a man identified with the most extreme anti-Arab attitude, meant of course that the government had decided the attack must be started immediately. While Nasser sat back under the illusion that his latest maneuvers had relieved the tension, final adjustments in the Israeli war plan were made. The army was ready to strike.

On assuming his new post, Dayan said, alluding to the enmity between him and Eshkol, "It took 80,000 Egyptian soldiers to put me here." It was literally true. Nasser, by a series of miscalculations, had succeeded in pushing Israel into a war he did not want, and which he could not win.

Yet, reviewing Nasser's actions during this crisis, one is struck by the inevitability of everything he did, as well as the inevitability of the Israeli reaction—because all of this had happened before, time and again, since the beginning of the century. Viewed as a story by itself, the events leading up to this war, in which tens of thousands of Arabs and seven hundred Israelis perished, may sound ludicrous. But viewed as just another chapter in the history of the past three generations in the Middle East, it could hardly have happened otherwise. It is necessary, therefore, to examine this history, to analyze and grasp its inner meaning, in order to understand why this war happened—and how its astonishing results may influence the future.

PART ONE

The Vicious Circle

3: Rudyard Kipling Meets Tolstoy

ONE DAY after the Six-Day War, I was told that Yulik had been killed during the attack on the Syrian hills. It came as a shock.

I hadn't seen Yulik for fifteen years. I remember him as a six-year-old child, not strikingly beautiful, but immensely alive, his face covered with freckles, speaking a rich Hebrew that would have sounded improbable coming from anyone but a *kibbutz* child.

My first question on hearing the news was, "How did Grysha and Nadia take it?" I was told that they took it as would be expected, not showing any sign of grief, seeming to comfort those who came to comfort them.

Grysha and Nadia are Yulik's parents. I used to know them when I was friendly with Yulik's sister, and she would take me home to her *kibbutz* sometimes during the Jewish festivals. They must have been shocked that their daughter went around with a fellow like me— not only a city boy but notorious for claiming to be, incredibly, an anti-Zionist. Not to be a Zionist must have seemed as curious to them as declaring oneself not to be a human being. But because I was their guest, they insisted upon accompanying me to the communal dining room at all the meals, shielding me from hostile looks of the other *kibbutz* members, who were as much bewildered as they to find such a strange animal in their midst.

During the frugal meals, always poor and always badly cooked, I kept looking at Grysha and Nadia and asking myself what made them tick. What made Nadia, who looked a lady from St. Petersburg high society, leave her home as a young girl, go alone to a far and desolate country and spend a lifetime of incredible hardship? What made Grysha, a young student somewhere in the Ukraine, leave everything and become a common laborer in the malaria-ridden valley of Ezreel? For me, they represent Zionism at its best. They were among the founders of the *kibbutz* at the end of World War I. For the first twenty years it was a life of sheer poverty, of back-breaking work, of unending sacrifice in a remote outpost surrounded by often hostile Arab villages, without even the smallest luxuries such as one's own clothing or any kind of privacy.

By the time I got to know them, the *kibbutz* was already quite well off, however, shaded by green trees, with its standard of living approaching that of the city. But, unlike most *kibbutzim*, this one refused to make the slightest concession to a better life. The food remained frugal, more as a matter of principle, I suspect, than out of necessity. Grysha was still working ten or twelve hours a day, doing all manner of manual labor. Nadia was still the *kibbutz* nurse, as untiring in her work as she was in the Twenties, when she would be seen riding on a cart bringing a woman in labor to the hospital in Affulah. Their first son, a youngster unusually gifted in music, followed in their footsteps. One day he put his violin on top of the cupboard never to touch it again, knowing that the *kibbutz* needed tractor drivers, not musicians. Their daughter, who could not stand *kibbutz* life, drifted into town and later married a Scandinavian U.N. observer. Having her leave the country to live in Europe must have been a shock to her parents. The death of the youngest child seemed somehow preordained. One would expect the son of such a couple, brought up in this atmosphere, to be in the front line, storming the Syrian fortifications which had tormented the *kibbutzim* along the frontier for so many years.

* * *

Zionism was a revolution like few in history.

Today, the word revolution may mean admitting a Negro into a swimming pool or changing the ownership of the factories or replacing one set of politicians with another. As deeply as they changed the lives of their peoples, how much did the great revolutions of our century—the Bolshevik, the Chinese, the Egyptian, the Cuban, the Algerian—actually affect the daily life of the individual?

Zionism was incomparably more revolutionary. It sent people from one country into another; a completely different one. It transferred people from one social class to another, usually a much lower one. It changed their language, their environment, their culture. It completely cut them off from their former lives and had them build others. Such a revolution is rare in human history. Looking for a precedent even remotely similar, one can think only of the First Crusade or the voyage of the Pilgrim Fathers. Big historical movements like these, changing the course of history and the face of the earth, must be viewed as a whole. It is quite futile to analyze them, to try to dissect them, laying bare just a few of their characteristics, and imagine that you have reached the heart.

Yet even a movement like this is a child of its time and its place. In order to understand Zionism, one has to realize when it was born and where. Officially, Zionism was born at the end of the last century, the invention of one man, Theodor Herzl, a bearded Viennese journalist. His picture, resembling an Assyrian king of antiquity, hangs opposite my seat in the *Knesset*, the only decorative element in the entire hall.

Herzl was trying to find a solution to the plight of the Jews in Europe. As a journalist in France, he was deeply impressed by the anti-Semitic outrages there during the Dreyfus affair. He formed the belief that Jews would never be able to find a place within the European community, and that, therefore, they had to form a nation of their own. Thus Zionism was a direct product of the spirit of nationalism in nineteenth-century Europe.

At a time when the idea of nationalism was all-conquering, when it reached and engulfed even the most backward peoples in Eastern Europe, it also reached the Jews. These Jews were not a nation in the usual sense of living together in a territory and having the outward signs usually attributed to a nation. Herzl decided to provide them with the attributes artificially, giving them first a sense of nationality and then a territory in which to live a national life. One could say that Zionism, as such, was the last of the national movements of Europe. It began to emerge and gather momentum just when the older nationalisms of Western and Central Europe had passed their peak, when nationalism, as a manifestation of Western Culture, as a response to economic and political challenges, was slowly becoming anachronistic. All around, fierce new national movements were raising their heads in Eastern Europe. Poles, Czechs, Slovaks, Serbs, Croatians, Lithuanians, and many others were clamoring for nationhood and independence, each dreaming of a small homogeneous nation-state of its own, where its own language and its own culture would reign supreme.

In these new nation-states, as yet unrealized, there was no place for the Jews. They did not belong. They were different. And so there was something highly appealing to Jews in the idea of leaving it all and creating a Jewish nation-state.

One of the peculiarities of the time was that each one of these new national movements tried to resurrect, and, if necessary, to invent, a glorious national history of its own. Each new state was conceived as a reincarnation of ancient glories, of the resurrection of some ancient state or empire in which that particular people had stamped its imprint on history. It was, therefore, quite natural for the early Zionists to think of a Jewish national home as solving more than the immediate problem—the plight of the Jews in modern, nationalistic Europe—and to think of a new state as a continuation of ancient Jewish history, after a short interruption of two thousand years. The old Israelite kingdoms constituted the first Jewish commonwealth, centered on the first Temple. After the return from Babylonian exile, the second Jewish commonwealth was set up, centered on the Second Temple. The time had come to create a new commonwealth, a modern Jewish state, in truth a Third Temple. Thus, the political idea, designed primarily to provide the European Jews with a haven of salvation, became imbued with a religious mystique that gave it a deep messianic impulse. Although all this was quite alien to Herzl himself, a typical Jewish-Viennese intellectual, when he came into contact with the Jewish masses in Eastern Europe, he became convinced that this mystique was essential to the movement.

* * *

Another spirit was abroad in Eastern Europe at that time, the spirit of socialism, the utopian myth that promised the liberation of man from the yoke of an oppressive social environment. For young Jews in the ghettos the gospel of Tolstoy and the gospel of Marx became intertwined. Labor, manual labor as a salvation for the soul, had a magical attraction for those boys and girls in Poland and Russia who saw their pale parents in the ghetto, the despised tailors and shopkeepers and money lenders.

All these diverse longings and aspirations resolved into one: to get away from it all, not to be any longer a helpless minority, at the mercy of any passing Cossack troop, any drunken mob of *mujiks* incited by a corrupt government incapable of providing them with any other outlet for their miseries but a bloody pogrom. To get away from a parasitical existence that made you despise yourself, your body and your work. To go somewhere where you would be master of your own fate. To till the soil and become free in mystical contact with mother earth. To create a society without masters and slaves, where everyone would be equal, where no one would be rich or poor. To do all this in your own state, in your own homeland, to follow in the footsteps of the ancient heroes of your people, to resurrect a Jewish commonwealth, to live where the events of the Bible actually took place. This was the dream.

It was a dream so beautiful, so basic, so tangible, it drew the best, the most adventurous, from all over Eastern Europe to a tiny far-off Turkish colony called Palestine.

It was a glorious movement of liberation, pure and simple, its aim to create a society untainted by any struggle except the struggle with its own soul.

Just one fact was completely overlooked in the excitement: Palestine was not an empty country.

* * *

The story of Zionism begins with a little book, written by Herzl in a mood of feverish excitement, that appeared in February, 1896. He called it *Der Judenstaat*, "The Jewish State," and it struck the Jewish masses in Europe like a thunderbolt. Coming at exactly the right time, in exactly the right mood, providing answers to questions on everybody's mind, it was one of those few documents which have changed the course of history. In this book, Herzl set down a complete, detailed blueprint of the future Jewish state. It contained such chapters as "Workers' Dwellings," "Purchase of Land," "Unskilled Laborers"; it described what the flag should look like; it told how the project was to be financed and dealt with many other topics.

But the book did not contain one single reference to the fact that Palestine was inhabited by Arabs. In fact, the word "Arab" does not appear in the book at all. As strange as it may seem, there was a reason for this: when Herzl dreamed about his state-to-be he did not think about it in terms of any particular country. His was a blueprint for a national home that could be set up anywhere—in Argentina, in Canada, in Uganda. Only during the last phase of writing his book did Herzl become convinced that the idea of Palestine might give the project of a Jewish state the necessary emotional thrust. Because of this he inserted a small passage into his book, saying that Palestine might be the best of the potential sites for the new Jewish state. In this passage, which sounds rather like an afterthought, he said that a Jewish state in Palestine would constitute "a part of the rampart of Europe against Asia," adding, "We would serve as an outpost of culture against barbarism." These words, put down perhaps without much thought, are highly significant. Herzl at that time had obviously thought very little about Palestine as a concrete entity. Probably he knew very little about it, about its inhabitants and geo-political significance. The phrases he used were just unconscious echoes of the spirit of the times.

In the Zionist Congress of 1931 an interesting description of Herzl's evolution was given by Chaim Weizmann, who was to become the first President of Israel, in a speech opposing demands to set the "final aim" of Zionism as a Jewish state. "In all of Herzl's declarations," said Weizmann, "the idea of the Jewish State appears only in his book, *Der Judenstaat*. When he wrote this book, Herzl was far from certain that Palestine was the land where his plan would probably be realized."

On the contrary, contended Weizmann, "Herzl thought about the Palestinian plan as something academic, as a pious wish not meriting serious consideration. There is no certainty whatsoever that his vision of a Jewish state applied to Palestine. The whole style of his book makes it probably that while writing it he was thinking about another land (Argentina), and that he added the passage about Palestine later on, just to make his Zionist friends feel good."

Weizmann points out that at the First Zionist Congress in 1897, when Herzl definitely joined the Zionist movement, "and thereby accepted the idea of Palestine as the land of Jewish resurrection, the formula of a Jewish state disappeared from his plan." The Zionist program, adopted by that Congress, speaks only about "a legally secured Jewish home in Palestine."

Those times were the heyday of imperialism, which had not yet become a despicable term, a synonym for exploitation and oppression. It was still a glorious concept, imbued with idealism. People were praising Rudyard Kipling's poetry glorifying the white man's burden. Cecil Rhodes, in South Africa, was the symbol of the European superman, a hero to one and all. No one even dreamed about the awakening of Asia and Africa, about the new nationalism of the East. The black man and the brown man were but "natives," barbarians (against whom Europe had to be defended) who merely happened to inhabit places where European nations sent their ships—and armies—for raw materials to supply the necessities of the burgeoning Industrial Revolution.

Thus, in time and place, Zionism at its inception was not only a part of the last wave of European nationalism, it was a part of the last wave of European imperial expansion. Soon, very soon, this wave would expend itself. Within less than ten years the Japanese were to inflict a terrible defeat on the Russians, bringing to an end the era of undisputed white supremacy.

Perhaps it was a misfortune of Zionism to be born too near the crossroads—a hundred years too late to profit by the great European expansionary movement, thirty years too early to recognize the impending force of Afro-Asian reaction to its arrival in Arab-inhabited Palestine.

The Zionists who congregated in Basel in 1897 for the First Zionist Congress were deeply conscious of taking part in a unique historical event. Except for a handful, these more or less self-appointed delegates of the Jewish people had never been to Palestine, had no idea what it was like and took little interest in its realities. Reality did not bother them. They were out to build a new world, only half imagined. The only reality they knew was one they wanted to get away from—the reality of Eastern Europe, with its pogroms, its discrimination, its forebodings of greater catastrophes to come. For this reason the early Zionists did not come to grips with the actual problems awaiting them in Palestine. They knew dimly that some people were living there; they vaguely felt that something should be done about them sometime; but it all seemed too vastly unimportant at that pregnant moment.

Herzl himself visited Palestine for the first time long after he published *Der Judenstaat* and convened the Congress itself. His main purpose in going to Palestine in the fall of 1898 was not to acquaint himself with the place where his ideas were to be realized, as one might have imagined, but to meet the German Kaiser Wilhelm II in an appropriately dramatic setting. Yet he must have realized by that time that some place must be found for the Arab natives in his grand design. In his second book, *Altneuland*, the "Old-New-Land," there appears an Arab gentleman, perfectly delighted to be living in a Jewish community, complimenting the Jews on their idealistic determination to grant the natives full equality after they had themselves suffered so much abroad.

I have often wondered how different Zionism might have been had Herzl not been a Viennese journalist but a shopkeeper in a Damascus bazaar. Would Zionism have realized that Palestine was a part of a big area inhabited by Arabs? Might some solution have been found at the very beginning to the problem of co-existence with the people who considered Palestine their own homeland? But these are, of course, idle thoughts. Herzl could not have been anything but a European Jew, because his whole idea was a response to a specific challenge posed by European conditions. And if Herzl had not been there, the great need of Eastern European Jewry would have produced some other apostle who would have provided the same kind of answers.

This was actually put to the test. Herzl died of a heart attack on July 3, 1904, at the age of 44. Near the end of his short life, disappointed at the failure of his efforts to acquire a charter establishing a Jewish state in Palestine, Herzl turned his attention to other potential sites. For some time his interest centered on the area of El-Arish in northern Sinai—one of the territories conquered by the Israeli Army in the 1967 war. When this project seemed unrealistic because of the lack of water in the area, he favored the acceptance of an offer in 1903 by the British government to settle the Jews on three thousand square miles in, of all places, Uganda. His stand shocked the masses of Eastern European Zionists; it was repudiated with contempt. (One wonders how the recent war would have looked if Ugandian Israel, facing the animosity of a black Africa, would have found itself fighting the armies of an African League!)

Born when and where it was, Zionism could not have
developed any differently. It was completely preoccupied with itself, with its great national and social vision,
with the dangers facing European Jews. It was too preoccupied with problems in countries Zionism wanted to
leave—in violent debates with assimilationists, Communists and other rivals—to bother with the still
largely unknown land where the new Jerusalem was to
be built.

Choosing their symbols, the Zionists looked to the
past of the Jewish people, not to the landscape of Palestine. Zion, though only a little hill in Jerusalem, was a
religious symbol, the place whence would come the
word of God. The *magen David*, the shield of David,
which became the emblem of the movement, was a
symbol taken from the synagogue and the graveyard.
The flag, a white cloth with blue stripes, was an adapta-
tion of the *talith*, the Jewish prayer mantle. Much later,
when the new State of Israel was looking for a coat of
arms, it chose the *menorah*, the seven-armed candle-
stick of the Temple. In all this world of symbols there
was no place for the non-Hebrew periods of the history
of Palestine, nor for the glorious heritage of the other
great Semitic sister-nations. Zionist nationalism just did
not blend into the landscape of the region, or even of
Palestine, with its many-splendored past. Today this
may seem strangely lacking in foresight, but at the time
it was quite natural, so natural, in fact, that it could
hardly have been different.

* * *

This, then, was the movement that slowly began to
infiltrate into Palestine toward the end of the last century, the first *aliyah* (wave of immigration) settling

there even before the birth of the Zionist movement itself, the second *aliyah*, composed of young socialists, following that event during the early years of the new country.

And in Palestine Zionism collided with a reality it was wholly unprepared to meet.

4: Old Jews and
Young Turks

AN OLD American movie depicting the early struggles of the American railways shows, in a memorable scene, how two trains manned by mercenaries of rival robber barons started to move from opposite directions on the same track, headed for eventual collision. Something like this was happening in Palestine. While the first prophets of Zionism were writing their books in Eastern Europe, Arab poets and young intellectuals were dreaming a dream of their own—the dream of the Arab nations' awakening and rising, throwing off the yoke of the Abominable Turk, restoring the glories of old.

A Jew named Moses Hess wrote a book called *Rome and Jerusalem*, a forerunner of Zionism, in 1862. Six years later, in 1868, the Arab poet Ibrahim Yazeji, at a secret meeting of the so-called Syrian Scientific Society, uttered the stirring cry, "Arise, ye Arabs, and awake!" In 1880 revolutionary posters appeared on the walls of Beirut demanding independence for Syria (including Palestine) and carrying the slogan, "by the sword may distant aims be attained, seek with it if you mean to succeed." In 1882 Leo Pinsker published his book *Auto-Emancipation*, another milestone on the road to Zionism.

While young Jewish intellectuals gathered in feverish meetings all over Central and Eastern Europe to plan for their adventurous new life in Palestine, Arab officers in the Turkish Army and Arab intellectuals in Beirut and Damascus were holding clandestine meetings, plotting against the Turks and looking for ways to achieve Arab independence. Neither faction had the slightest idea of the existence of the other.

Here some of the great "if onlys" of history interpose themselves. What would have happened if only the Zionists, somehow foreseeing the great Afro-Asian revolution of the new century, had identified themselves with its spirit? If only they had seen themselves as an ancient Semitic people returning to its homeland, imbued with brotherly love for the Semitic people inhabiting the region? If only they had turned themselves into the leaders of a great national revolution in the Middle East, the spearhead of the region's fight against foreign domination and imperialism? A generation later it might have happened. But at the turn of the century Arab nationalism was a mere seed hidden in the soil, unsuspected by the superficial observer, especially an observer looking at the landscape from far-away Europe.

* * *

Arab nationalism was a simple idea. It was not faced with the immensely complicated problems which confronted Zionism. There was no question of moving a people, creating a new language, organizing a new society. The Arabs were at least living on their own land, tilling their own soil, even if they were subjugated by the governors and soldiers of a degenerate colonial empire. All they had to do was to rise against their Ottoman Turkish masters, liberate their territory and create one great Arab state, or a set of Arab states.

For hundreds of years Arab society had been stagnant. The vital energy which had propelled the Arabs out of the deserts, creating a great Arab empire, producing a great Arab culture, had long since spent itself. A new impetus was needed if Arabs were to become again a living force in history. This impetus was provided by nationalism.

Nationalism is, of course, a specific manifestation of the spirit of Western culture. By embracing nationalism the peoples of Asia and Africa adopted Western ways in order to regain their place in a world in which Western culture, Western technology and Western military techniques reigned supreme. Zionism, as we have seen, was the last national movement born within the framework of Western culture. Arab nationalism, born at the same time, was one of the first national movements born outside this framework. Nationalism, after fulfilling its mission in Europe, and becoming obsolescent there, was commencing its historical march across the deserts and jungles and steppes of Asia and Africa.

At the beginning of this century about half a million Arabs lived in Palestine. The Jewish population, which amounted to 24,000 in 1882, rose to 50,000 by the end of the century and 85,000 as World War I began. These two populations viewed each other with mixed feelings, not quite knowing how to treat one another, maneuvering rather like sparring partners before the big match.

The first Jewish settlers in their isolated villages, surrounded by the Arab countryside, wavered between an attitude of friendliness and cooperation and a policy of toughness and contempt. As soon as one wave of settlers got used to its environment, learned the Arab's language and habits, made contact with neighboring villages and employed Arab labor, a new wave of immigrants fresh from Eastern Europe would upset this uneasy relationship, taking over Arab employment in the Jewish villages and adopting the idea that you have to be tough to the Arabs to command their respect. More or less the same thing happened on the Arab side. At times the village chiefs would deal with the Jewish settlements in a friendly way, realizing the economic advantages to be gained thereby, only to be accused the next day by other Arabs of aiding and abetting the infiltration of the land by foreigners who might eventually take it over.

Arguments over land, wells and employment would erupt from time to time, poisoning the atmosphere. Such bickering was commonplace among the Arabs but upsetting to the Jews, who had been brought up differently. The inroads made by the Bedouins, who have made sporadic attacks on the villages of Palestine since the dawn of history, further aggravated the situation. But on the whole, no real hostility developed. Most Jewish settlers looked upon the Arabs as a part of the landscape without much significance, as occasional laborers, as the ones who brought the fruit to town. Most Arabs must have considered the Jews curious additions to the landscape, too few to make any great difference. It was only when the relationship started to reach the political level that the shape of things to come emerged.

At the beginning of the century a new spirit was

abroad throughout the Turkish empire. The Turkish
Sultan Abd-el-Hamid, who foresaw that nationalism
would break up the multi-national empire of the Otto-
mans, and who therefore brutally suppressed any nationalistic manifestations of the Arabs, was repudiated
by the rising of the Young Turks; these were Turkish
nationalists. The success of the Young Turks gave hope
to the Arab nationalists. They believed that Turkish
reformers would change the structure of the Ottoman
Empire, giving the Arabs at least some form of auton-
omy and national expression. These hopes were quickly
dashed. The Turkish generals and politicians who took
over the moribund empire, vainly trying to heal the Sick
Man of Europe, had no intention whatsoever of recognizing any nationalism but their own.

It was at that time that the first political contact was
established between Arabs and Zionists. By itself a
small and passing phase, its significance was profound.

* * *

The intrigues and struggles within the Ottoman Empire provided the Zionist leadership with their first real
choice. Should they support the Arabs against the
Turks, or the Turks against the Arabs? Among those
Zionist functionaries who resided in Palestine and in
Constantinople, the Ottoman capital, some new ideas
were timidly aired. The feasibility of a pact with the
Arabs in their fight against the Turkish monster was
dimly realized by a few. Yet their opinions, recorded in
letters and reports of the period, carried little weight
within the Zionist leadership, residing as it did in Europe and looking upon affairs in the "Orient" from a
superior vantage point of world politics. The Pales-

tinian segment of Zionism was as yet small and secondary. The base of the movement, the masses of its
followers, the seat of its institutions, were all still in
Europe, seeing these affairs through European eyes. (In
passing, one cannot help but wonder why the leadership
of the movement was not transferred immediately to
Palestine, the land which was the sole object of all
Zionism's aims and endeavors. The reason was, of
course, that the colonization effort was still viewed as
only a secondary aspect of the movement. The main
objective was to acquire the international charter for
the establishment of a national home in Palestine.
What's more, the majority of Zionist leaders, then as
now, did not really relish the prospect of transferring
themselves to an environment vastly inferior to the one
in which they were living.)

The official doctrine was enunciated time and again
by Max Nordau, the famous German-Jewish writer who
became the most outstanding personality of the movement upon the death of Herzl in 1904. Martin Buber
recounts, in one of his books, how Nordau, upon hearing for the first time that there were Arabs living in
Palestine, ran to Herzl, deeply shocked, exclaiming, "I
didn't know that! We are committing an injustice!"
However, Nordau seems to have recovered from his
shock handsomely. In his address to the Seventh Zionist
Congress, which convened in Basel in 1905, he said,

The movement which has taken hold of a great part of the
Arab people may easily take a direction which may cause
harm in Palestine. . . . The Turkish government may feel
itself compelled to defend its reign in Palestine, in Syria,
against its subjects by armed power. . . . In such a position,
Turkey might become convinced that it may be important
for her to have, in Palestine and Syria, a strong and well

organized people which, with all respect to the rights of
the inhabitants living there, will resist any attack on the
authority of the Sultan and defend this authority with all
its might.

This was, quite clearly, a direct offer to turn the Zionist
settlement into a bastion for the Turkish government,
against the inhabitants of the country. It meant, practically speaking, a declaration of war on the emerging
Arab nationalist movement.

A far-reaching decision indeed, yet it was arrived at
quite naturally, even automatically. It was not inspired, as it might seem now, by any enmity toward the
Arabs and their aspirations, nor even by any sympathy
toward imperialism. It was simply an outcome of the
particular situation in which Zionism found itself. As
Nordau himself put it four years later, addressing the
Ninth Zionist Congress in Hamburg following the Revolt of the Young Turks,

The land of our hopes, our aspirations and our efforts, the
Holy Land of our fathers, is within the boundaries of the
Ottoman Empire. Its shores and its frontiers are guarded
by Turkish soldiers. The keys of the house which the
Zionists want to turn into their national home are in the
hands of the Turkish government. It is, therefore, natural
that all our endeavors turn themselves toward Turkey,
much as the needle of the compass turns toward the
magnetic pole.

A different policy, such as was advocated by some faint
Zionist voices in Constantinople, would have meant
antagonizing the Turkish government, closing the doors
of Palestine to Jewish immigration perhaps forever.
Zionist leaders in Europe could not foresee that within a
few years the Ottoman Empire would break up and the

Arab nations assume an importance as yet undreamed of. Yet even had they foreseen this, could they have acted differently? Could they have exposed the embryonic Jewish settlements to the crushing vengeance of a brutal Turkish government, could they have risked a possible discontinuation of Jewish immigration, all to establish a relationship with the Arabs which might or might not have borne fruit at some future time? Could they, in short, have let go of the bird in hand for the two in the bush?

A thoroughly imaginative leadership, statesmen endowed with the political foresight of a Bismarck or a Lenin, might have risked such a course, trusting in the accuracy of their intuition or analysis. The Zionist leaders of the time were simply unprepared for such a role. They took the easiest and most obvious course.

* * *

In a less obvious way, the Arabs were faced with a similar dilemma. Should they resist the Jewish settlement by any available means, or should they try to make a pact with the Jews in order to gain their assistance in their fight against the Turks?

Several Arab leaders in Palestine, then and later, advocated the latter course. They tried to make contact with Jewish leaders to work out a basis for cooperation. (At that time it was not yet considered treason to the Arab cause.) A few months before Nordau made his speech to the Ninth Zionist Congress in 1909, setting a strictly pro-Turkish course, the Zionist delegate in Constantinople had had a series of conversations with the two Jerusalemite Arab deputies in the new Turkish Parliament. He had reported to the President of the Zionist organization that one of them had put great emphasis on the common interests of the Jews and Arabs, their common Semitic origin and their opposition to the Turks. Such views were by no means unusual at the time. In actuality, various Arab National Committees in Beirut and Cairo discussed proposals for a basis of cooperation, looking upon Jewish immigration to Palestine as a repatriation of authentic Syrians, much like the Arab Syrians who had emigrated during the nineteenth century to the United States and Latin America. It is difficult to assess today the importance of these sentiments and of the leaders who voiced them. They might have been a minority. There is no certainty whatsoever that the Arab national movement would have accepted ideas like these had they actually been embraced by the Zionist movement. The choice had never to be made anyway, because no such concrete proposal was ever put forward by the Zionist headquarters in Europe.

Up until World War I, which created a completely new situation, the Arab attitude was, on the whole, indecisive. There certainly was no resolute, clear-cut opposition to Jewish immigration and settlement, neither by political means nor by armed resistance. This came much later. It seems, therefore, that until World War I, there still existed a definite possibility of merging Zionism and Arab nationalism into one great movement—a possibility never tested, and not even seriously explored.

Analyzing this period, and many similar chapters in the later history of Palestine, one must realize that on the whole it was the Zionists who could have taken the initiative, being a new force on the Palestinian scene. Zionists were acting, the Arabs were reacting. It was, therefore, the Zionists who made the choices—often consciously but more often unconsciously—while the Arabs, faced with this new and foreign element, could only respond to situations not of their own making. But, in all justice, viewing the events in historical perspective, the Zionists can hardly be blamed. Fully occupied with their heroic struggle to gain a foothold in a new country, to turn young intellectuals into hardworking farmers, to create the first embryonic armed force for self-defense, to fight disease and hunger, they still viewed the Arab question as something of lesser importance, perhaps hoping that by ignoring the problem it would go away.

* * *

While the question of dealing with the Arabs on the scene was taken lightly, the Zionist leaders were engrossed in their efforts to gain the support of at least one world power. Herzl himself never dreamed of establishing his Jewish state by a simple *fait accompli*. He was thinking in terms of the great colonial enterprises, the chartered companies. His dream was to turn the movement into one great chartered company, different from all the others, not owned by capitalists bent on exploitation, but the property of a whole people striving to put its roots down. It was a beautiful idea, imposing in its naïveté.

The First Zionist Congress had called for "a legally secured Jewish home in Palestine." Secured, that meant, by a charter from the family of nations, or by some world power. Herzl saw his life work as the securing of this charter, and so did his successors. The first person to address was, obviously, the Turkish Sultan. Herzl himself tried to convince Abd-el-Hamid, quite oblivious to the fact that this bloody potentate was uni-

versally hated by his Arab subjects as a brutal oppres-
sor. Herzl went to Constantinople and was received by
the Sultan on May 17, 1901, not as a Zionist delegate
but as a journalist. In a two-hour conversation he
offered the Sultan the assistance of world Jewry in solving Turkey's chronic financial difficulties. Later Herzl
met several other high-ranking Ottoman officials, reit-
erating the same idea.

When these efforts proved futile, the obvious next
person to address was the German Kaiser, by that time
the foremost ally of the Turks. Germany stood at the
peak of its imperial aspirations and endeavors. The
Drang nach Osten, the eastward urge, led to the plan
for a Berlin-to-Baghdad railway as part of an effort to
fill the Middle Eastern vacuum with German imperial
power. As early as 1895 Herzl had written to Reichs-
kanzler Otto von Bismarck a letter in which he said:
"If my program is too premature, I put it at the disposal of the German government. May it use it when it
sees fit to do so."

During his visit to Turkey and the Holy Land, Kaiser
Wilhelm, on horseback, received Herzl near the Jewish
village of Mikve-Israel, on the road from Jerusalem to
Jaffa, on November 2, 1898. Herzl asked the Kaiser to
become the patron of the Zionist settlement organization in Palestine and Syria. Wilhelm did not commit
himself, but expressed his appreciation of both the
German and the Jewish colonies established in the
country. "Your movement," he said, "is based on a
sound idea."

What could be more suitable than to offer the German Kaiser the prospect of a European community established in Palestine at the crossroads of the Orient as
an outpost of German interests and culture? Herzl was

quite certain that German would be the language of the new community anyhow. (He did not believe in the extraordinary experiment of resurrecting the Hebrew language, dead for two thousand years; that miracle, no part of the Zionist plan, became a major ingredient of the movement only when the new settlers in Palestine, eager to begin a life in the footsteps of the ancient Israelites, shed their old languages, including Yiddish, which symbolized life in the Diaspora. Hebrew, the language born in the country, so similar to the Arabic spoken there, was the ideal symbol of all they were striving for.) The Kaiser, a pathetically inadequate figure, given to fad and fashions and to diverse extravagant poses, toyed for a time with the idea of becoming the patron of the new Temple, the saviour of the Jewish race, but he was an anti-Semite at heart and saw himself as a potential Sword of Islam, so the fancy quickly passed.

In desperation Herzl turned to the British. The man who lent him an ear was the very archetype of the British imperialist. Joseph Chamberlain, the legendary colonial secretary, with uncanny foresight, it seems, realized the potential of Zionism as a means of furthering British overseas interests. His offer to create a Jewish settlement in northern Sinai was a part of a British plan to extend the frontiers of Egypt northward into Palestine to gain greater depth for the defense of the Suez Canal. The objective of nearly every Egyptian ruler, from the ancient pharaohs to Gamal Abd-el-Nasser, was to gain a foothold in Palestine to prevent hostile penetration of the Sinai Desert which might then threaten the Nile Valley. Chamberlain, with Britain's possession of Egypt and the Suez Canal, thought that Zionism might help him block any potential Turkish-

German threat. It was the exact opposite of the objective that had appealed to the Kaiser when he briefly considered using Zionism for German interests.

The idea of a Jewish commonwealth in Palestine as an outpost for the British Empire was by no means new. In 1840 this idea was promoted by Lord Palmerston, who thought that a Jewish settlement in the Holy Land would help the Ottoman Empire, then supported by the British, against the Egyptians, who were supported by the French.

Palmerston wrote to his ambassador in Constantinople: "There exists at the present time among the Jews dispersed over Europe, a strong notion that the time is approaching when their nation is to return to Palestine. . . . The Jewish people, if returning under the sanction and protection and at the invitation of the Sultan, would be a check upon any future evil designs of Mehemet Ali or his successor. . . . I have to instruct Your Excellency strongly to recommend [to the Turkish Government] to hold out every just encouragement to the Jews of Europe to return to Palestine." These were the very same arguments used 60 years later by Herzl and his successors. Mehemet Ali, the Egyptian dictator, was, in a way, the forerunner of the modern Arab national movement.

On August 17, 1840, there appeared an editorial in the *Times* of London, recommending a plan "to plant the Jewish people in the land of their fathers." This plan was advanced by Lord Ashley (later Lord Shaftesbury). The rights and privileges of the settlement were to be "secured to them under the protection of a European power." The power hinted at was, of course, Britain.

Herzl died without realizing his aim in Palestine—or

Sinai or Uganda. For a few years no new opportunities presented themselves. The Zionist ship stood becalmed until the great storm broke. World War I launched Zionism as a force in world politics.

* * *

On November 2, 1917, the Zionists achieved the aim they had been working toward since the first day of the movement. They got their charter.

Many books have been written about the Balfour Declaration, in which His Majesty's Government promised to establish a national home for the Jews in Palestine. Many reasons have been given: the deep attachment of the British to the Holy Book; the need to win over American Jewry to help get the United States into the war on the side of the Allies; the effort to prevent Russian Jews from turning Bolshevik and quitting the war; even the wish to reward Dr. Chaim Weizmann for services rendered.

There may be some truth in all of these reasons, but essentially the Declaration was simply a pact between Great Britain and Zionism for the future of Palestine. In return for British assistance in Zionism's great colonization adventure, it undertook to provide Great Britain with a valid moral reason for keeping Palestine for itself, in spite of commitments the British had made to the French and the Arabs. (By the agreement reached by M. F. Georges-Picot, for France, and Sir Mark Sykes, for Great Britain, and officially recognized by notes exchanged in April-May 1916 between France, Great Britain and Russia, Syria was allotted to France; Iraq and Transjordan, with Southern Palestine, to Britain; but North and Central Palestine, excluding the Haifa Bay, but including Jerusalem, Jaffa and Gaza, were turned into an international zone. Later, in February, 1917, on the request of Sir Mark Sykes, some Zionist leaders, led by the veteran Nachum Sokoloff, met with Georges-Picot and tried to convince him to agree to the inclusion of Palestine in the British sphere.) France having become Britain's great rival in the Middle East, it was imperative that the British contain French influence there and get a strong grip on Palestine and Transjordan, which had become important not just as a base for guarding the Suez Canal, but as an outlet for Iraqi oil, as well.

Nothing ever caused so much bitterness in the Arab world as the Balfour Declaration. The Arabs still see it as a perfidious act of treason, as a flagrant breach of the promises given at the same time to the Arabs. Their profound conviction that Israel is a product of colonialism, a creation of the imperialists, also stems directly from the Balfour Declaration. This is, of course, a misconception. If Britain used Zionism for its colonial interests, she certainly was used by the Zionists for their own ends. The fruits that Britain reaped from this pact were transient; the fruits that Zionism gathered were permanent.

It is with the Balfour Declaration that the relationship between Zionism and the Arabs assumed its final shape. It was a story of the Young Turkish period all over again, but by now clearly defined. The Arabs saw great masses of foreign settlers streaming into the country—the third *aliyah*, bubbling with energy, establishing *kibbutzim* all over the country. They saw a new colonial regime presided over by a Jewish high commissioner sent from Britain, Sir Herbert Samuel, actively assisting the colonization. For the first time they took up arms as a people, beginning the series of armed clashes of which the Six-Day War in 1967 was but one more round—the seventh or the eighth. Defending itself, the *Yishuv*, as the Jewish state-within-a-state was called, set up its first nationwide military organization, the *Haganah* (meaning defense). The most extreme nationalist leaders, led by Vladimir Jabotinsky, demanded the setting-up of a Jewish legion within the British Army (three such battalions had served in the British Army during World War I and were disbanded after the war).

Thus began the cycle in which Zionist-Arab relations have moved incessantly ever since: (1) The Zionists increase their efforts at immigration and settlement; (2) the Arabs react violently to what they consider a mortal threat to their national existence; (3) to contain the threat and gain political and military assistance, the Zionists look for an ally, an ally that can only be a foreign power whose interests are being adversely affected by the rising Arab nationalism; (4) the pact between Zionism and the foreign power whets Arab hatred and bitterness, sharpening their attack upon the Jewish national home; (5) this increases for the Zionists the need for even bigger allies. It is a complete cycle, a truly vicious circle, this not-so-merry-go-round where each rider sits on his horse as it goes up and down, imagining that it is he who decides his course, tragically condemned—by the inner logic of his earlier acts and the ideology nourished by them—to follow a pre-destined course.

* * *

A half-hearted attempt to break out of the cycle was made immediately after World War I. If it had no great historical significance, it is titillating because it shows what could have been.

The undisputed leader of Zionism at the time was Dr. Chaim Weizmann. While most of the Zionist leaders at the beginning of the war were drawn toward Germany, partly because they detested czarist Russia, Weizmann threw in his lot with the British. With Britain victorious and the Balfour Declaration gained, the eminent scientist became the Grand Old Man of Zionism.

The leader emerging on the other side was Emir Faisal, one of the Hashemite princes who fought the Turks in the Arabian Desert. T. E. Lawrence, an agent of the Cairo Bureau which directed British imperial policy in the Middle East, tried to help Faisal become King of Syria.

Lawrence was fantically anti-French. Creating an Arab kingdom in Syria, under a king friendly to the British, was not only a means of fulfilling Lawrence's pro-Arab dreams, but also a clever way of cheating the French out of the Middle Eastern dominion which was promised them in the Sykes-Picot pact.

But for the Arabs, who never loved and admired the rather dubious Lawrence quite as much as he thought they did, it was not a question of choosing between two imperial evils. They wanted Syria, all of it, to become an independent kingdom, including Palestine, which they called Southern Syria. When they convened a great national congress at Damascus, some of them thought that an agreement with the Zionists should be sought, in order to combine the efforts of both Arabs and Jews for the liberation of the Middle East.

At the same time, Lawrence was trying to combine

Arab and Zionist influence for the benefit of exclusive British domination of the Middle East. A series of romantic meetings between Weizmann and Faisal was initiated with the idea of confronting the Peace Conference with the *fait accompli* of a Jewish-Arab agreement.

In theory, the Zionist leadership, at that time, could have allied Zionism to the Arab national movement. The mood was right, the Balfour Declaration could still have been interpreted by the Arabs in a different way. One outstanding Syrian leader officially offered the Zionists an autonomous Palestinian state federated with Syria under the Syrian crown. (Nearly thirty years later a very similar proposal was to be made by King Abdallah, Faisal's brother, on the eve of the setting-up of the State of Israel.) But the Zionist leadership, which finally moved to Palestine early in 1918, was quite unprepared for any such idea. Not one of its members had the slightest knowledge of Arab nationalism. The idea of resisting British imperialism would have looked to them at the time ridiculous.

The second way, the one advocated by Lawrence and his friends, seemed more attractive. Contact with Faisal was maintained. The Arab prince, a desert chieftain rather bewildered by the wiles of world diplomacy, was quite sympathetic to the idea of a Jewish commonwealth in Palestine under his crown. In his tribal world, race meant a great deal, and the idea that the Jews were true members of the Semitic family played a major part in his thinking. In one of his messages, quite incredible today, he apologized for not being able to take part in a Zionist conference for purely technical reasons, adding that such conferences were important for futhering the understanding between "the two nations which are linked by ancient ties." In a letter to American-Jewish leader Felix Frankfurter early in 1919 he said:

We know that the Arabs and the Jews are racial relatives. . . . We shall do everything we can, as far as it depends on us, to assist in the acceptance of the Zionist proposals by the Peace Conference, and we shall welcome the Jews with all our hearts on their return home. The Jewish movement is national and not imperialist, our movement is national and not imperialist, and in Syria there is a place for both of us. Indeed, I think that neither of us can achieve real success without the other.

Two months before this, the famous Weizmann-Faisal agreement was drawn up under the auspices of Lawrence. In its preamble, it recognized the "racial kinship and the ancient bonds existing between the Arabs and the Jewish people," and expressed the realization that "the surest means of working out the consummation of their national aspirations is through the closest possible collaboration." The agreement pledged the support of the Zionist organization to a great Arab state, and Arab support to a state of Palestine, based on the Balfour Declaration. The agreement said that "all necessary measures shall be taken to encourage and stimulate immigration of Jews into Palestine on a large scale and as quickly as possible to settle Jewish immigrants upon the land." Significantly, any matter of dispute was to be referred to the British government for arbitration. The agreement never came into force, however. Faisal, who signed it without the authorization of his family, made the signature conditional on the acceptance of his claims for Syria by the Peace Conference. This, of course, never happened. The French attacked Damascus and drove Faisal, together with the Syrian and Palestinian nationalists, out of Syria.

The Zionists were not greatly distressed by this. Their claims were accepted in the Peace Settlement held at San Remo in April, 1920, and incorporated in the documents which established a British mandate over Palestine, ratified by the League of Nations in 1922. One feels that the Zionists were rather relieved at avoiding the necessity of dealing with the unfamiliar phenomenon of Arab nationalism and content to go back to their dealings with the British.

The whole intermezzo is interesting only as an indication of what could have been.

* * *

For nearly twenty years the British-Zionist relationship continued with many misgivings. British colonial officials could find no common language with Russian-Jewish leaders, but found some attachment for romantic Arab sheiks. The Arabs, accusing the British of turning their land over to the Jews, revolted every few years with ever-increasing violence. The Jews accused the British colonial administration, with increasing justification, of going back on their word, putting mounting obstacles in the way of Zionist fulfillment. Indeed, in May, 1939, the British restricted Jewish immigration to the barest minimum, forbidding outright the buying up of Arab land by the Jews in many parts of Palestine.

Great Britain had become uneasy at the sight of a white community growing up in Palestine, governing itself, keeping a well-organized underground army that posed a new threat to the dominance of Great Britain in the country. Extreme Jewish terrorists began attacking British installations. Their leader, Jabotinsky, an Anglophile to the core, still supported British imperialism; he sought to convince the British, by force of arms, that the Jews of Palestine would be a stronger and more capable ally for them than the Arabs. Only in 1940 did Abraham Stern, alias Yair, break away from Jabotinsky's *Irgun* group, create his own underground organization and proclaim the new revolutionary idea of fighting British imperialism as such.

Stern was captured and shot in the back by British police officers on the roof of an old building in Tel Aviv, but his ideas continued to gain ground. The *Irgun*, and later the official Zionist *Haganah*, joined the fight against the British mandate, until the British, in disgust or despair, shrewdly decided to leave the country, possibly with the idea that Palestine would be invaded and conquered by friendly Arab armies. This hope, if it ever existed, was confounded by the newly emerging army of Israel, which astounded the world by its military strength and agility.

The Jewish underground fight against the British colonial regime in Palestine was the first successful war of liberation in the Middle East. It makes a mockery of the idea that Zionism, or the State of Israel, was a puppet of imperialism and colonialism.

It also made a deep impression on the minds of the young generation of the Arab world, which saw that Britain could be attacked and vanquished. The most instructive lesson was given to the Arabs by two Israeli youths who were sent by the Stern organization to Cairo to kill the British Minister Resident, Lord Moyne. The two youngsters were captured, brought to trial before an Egyptian court, sentenced to death and executed by the unwilling Egyptians after Winston

Churchill expressly ordered them to do so. Speaking in Parliament at the end of February 1945, reporting on the recent Yalta conference, Churchill demanded that death sentences passed in Egypt for political murders should be executed, so as to serve as a warning to others. The stand of the two youngsters in court, however, was most extraordinary. They spoke against imperialism, disclaiming Zionism and declaring themselves patriots of Palestine. In his last statement before sentence was passed, Eliahu Beth-Zuri, one of the two accused, whom I knew in the *Irgun*, said "We, the Hebrews, who are the natural sons of the soil of Israel, fought for Palestine long before the Balfour Declaration. . . . My ideas are not the ideas of Zionism. We do not fight for the fulfillment of the Balfour Declaration. We do not fight for the National Home. We fight for our freedom." They made a profound impression on the young Egyptians plotting at the time the overthrow of their own British masters in Egypt. One of them, most certainly, was Gamal Abd-el-Nasser. Yet only some of the followers of Stern thought of themselves as fighters against imperialism as such or ever considered the possibility of a great anti-imperialist alliance of Arabs and Jews. For the official Zionist leadership and all the other Zionist groups and factions, this idea simply did not exist. Becoming convinced that further co-operation between Britain and Zionism had become impossible, they looked for another foreign ally, and found it in the even more powerful United States.

From the middle Forties onwards, the United States became the main ally of Zionism. For a short time, in 1947, the Soviet Union joined this alliance, mainly because it preferred a Jewish state to a colonial British military base which might have easily become a missile

base against the U.S.S.R. Under these political conditions, the United Nations resolved to partition Palestine
into a Jewish state and an Arab state. The Arab state of
Palestine never materialized, falling victim to the ambitions and intrigues of the neighboring Arab states. The
Jewish State of Israel was brought into being by force
of arms, against intense opposition.

The setting up of the state did not change the character of the vicious Arab-Jewish circle. The ever-present
and increasing threat of the surrounding Arab armies,
which never hid their intention of destroying the Jewish
state in "occupied Palestine," made it imperative for
the government of Israel to ally itself with as great a
power as possible. With certain brief interruptions, the
U.S.-Israeli alliance quickly became a dominant factor
in the Middle East. For a short time, this alliance was
overshadowed by the military cooperation between Israel and France. Faced with a war of liberation in Algeria, which they naïvely thought to be inspired and led
by the Egyptians, the French decided to open a second
front with the help of the Israelis. The Israeli Government was only too happy to use the French to gain its
own ends, and to acquire from them the arms needed
for a preventive war against Egypt. Thus, the joint Is-
raeli-French-British enterprise against Egypt was born
in 1956. Israel gained a brilliant victory, retained some
of its fruits, but confirmed deepening suspicions among
the Arabs concerning Israel's expansionist and colonial
character.

After the liberation of Algeria, the marriage of con-
venience between France and Israel became useless
from the French point of view and gradually cooled
until it was dramatically terminated by General de
Gaulle in December 1967. America again became Is-

rael's great ally, a fact which emerged clearly during the 1967 war, even though Israel fought and won alone, overshadowing its own prior victories.

* * *

An Arab, going over this brief history, can find in it enough to warrant the conclusion that Israel was created by imperialism, will always be aligned to it and couldn't exist without it. Yet, this conclusion is a misreading of the facts. Israel is the product of a great liberating movement, which by the peculiar circumstances of its inception was forced into imperialistic alliances, yet never was a puppet. Rather, it was a partner that retained the fruits of its cooperation long after the other partner had departed. It is imperative that the Arabs understand this for several reasons.

First of all, a misreading of the facts can lead to a dangerous misunderstanding of the reality. It is easy to feel contempt for a puppet, a contempt which may backfire when put to the test. It is also dangerous, since Israel is not a puppet, to assume that Israel will disappear once its imperialist patrons disappear from the Middle East. This is an illusion.

Secondly, the true character of Israel has to be recognized if ever an end is to be put to the Arab-Jewish vicious circle. Under a certain set of circumstances, Israel became an ally of imperialism, much as other states did. Under a different set of circumstances, Israel can and will assume a different posture. It may then mean something quite different to Arab nationalism.

It is important not only for the Arabs; the Israelis themselves must learn to analyze their recent past with complete objectivity in order to understand how their great progressive and liberating movement, one of the most glorious in history, came to be bound up with modern imperialism, one of the most unsavory of world movements.

Zionism was an authentic movement. No one created it but the Zionists themselves. There can be no real question about that, outside the realm of propaganda. Yet the question remains: What kind of movement was Zionism in the context of the history of Palestine?

5: Crusaders and Zionists

In September, 1967, on the seventieth anniversary of the First Zionist Congress, General Yitzhak Rabin was invited to address a commemorative meeting. It was held in the hall of the original congress in Basel. Toward the end of his speech, the victor of the Six-Day War startled everyone. He compared Israel to the Crusaders' Kingdom of Jerusalem and drew the conclusion that the main danger to Israel is the dwindling of immigration, much as the Crusaders' state decayed because of a lack of new blood.

To an outsider, this may not sound particularly startling, but for an Israeli, and a Chief of Staff at that, to compare Israel to the Crusaders approaches heresy. One reason for this is that the average Israeli learns very little about the Crusaders' two hundred-year stay in Palestine, but very much about what the Crusaders did on the way there. The atrocities committed by the Crusaders, and those who pretended to be Crusaders, in Southern Germany and elsewhere left an indelible imprint on Jewish history.

But there is a second reason. The Crusaders came to a bad end. After ceaseless fighting for eight consecutive generations, they were finally, literally, thrown into the sea. Israelis fear that the very analogy may cast an evil spell on their own historical experiment. For precisely the same reasons, Arabs like to compare the Zionists to the Crusaders, an "automatic" comparison of course quite childish; history doesn't repeat itself in quite this mechanical a fashion. The analogy between Israel and the Crusaders' kingdom of Jerusalem is interesting nevertheless, both for the similarities and the dissimilarities it reveals.

* * *

The Crusader bug bit me a few years after Israel's War of Liberation. I had rather casually started to read Steven Runciman's excellent *History of the Crusades.* Coming to the chapter about the fortifications the Crusaders built opposite the Gaza Strip to defend their kingdom against the Egyptians, I was suddenly struck by the idea that as a soldier in the Army of Israel I had occupied exactly the same positions.

As I continued my reading with a fresh eye, hundreds of large and small similarities sprang to mind. This can become an obsession. One begins to identify not only great events and institutions, but also personalities, kings, dukes and knights, wondering who is the Zionist prince of Galilee and who the duke of Transjordan.

The similarities are indeed striking. The Crusaders' movement, like the Zionist one, was a revolution so profound, so far-reaching, that it defies rational explanation. Of the many reasons attributed to this phenomenon—political, social, cultural—none is completely satisfactory.

The Crusaders, much as the Zionists, make one wonder what induces people suddenly to leave their homes and comfortable lives, marching for thousands of miles among innumerable perils to a distant and uninviting country, to live there in unending struggle, fighting unknown diseases and an implacable foe. What combination of glorious visions, selfless idealism, craving for loot, sheer disgust with the old life, and the promise of a new Jerusalem only dimly imagined, was needed to raise such a human tidal wave?

The Crusaders had their "Herzl" in Pope Urban. Their "First Zionist Congress" was their Council of Clermont, in November, 1095, eight hundred and two years before the historical gathering in Basel. The cry of "God wills it" echoes in the cry of "Let's go, Children of Jacob" which became the motto of the first Zionist *aliyah*.

Yet there was a significant difference in the conscious objectives of the two movements. The Crusaders went to Palestine to wrest the Holy Land from the hands of the Infidel. Settling in the land was only incidental to the necessity of guarding the holy places once regained. The ethos of the movement was anti-Moslem in its very essence. Zionism, on the contrary, was essentially a colonizing movement. The fight against the Arabs was only incidental, and, as we have seen, totally unexpected. The Zionists thought that Palestine was empty. The Crusaders went there because it was not empty. Yet these differences of motivation did not lead to vastly different results. Whether they wanted war or not, both movements had to fight, to settle the land, to guard its possessions.

Another difference is that the Crusaders came as conquerors, taking possession of the country in one big military campaign, settling on the land after their victory. The Zionists came as settlers, bought land piecemeal, set up their fortified villages and took over the country in a war they did not want after creating a base strong enough to sustain a sovereign state.

But both of these differences, important as they may be, are negligible compared with the striking similarity in the general direction of the two movements. Like the Philistines before them, they came from the west, partly by sea. Every seaborne invasion of Palestine has created the necessity of establishing a beachhead, fortifying it against the surrounding land, with supplies and reinforcements coming by ship. It creates, even unconsciously, a posture of facing the hostile hinterland with one's back to the sea as a secure base. Correspondingly, among the population of the surrounding area, it raises the spectre of foreign invasion by an alien body, to which the country has to react. In this the invasions from the west seem different, in the history of Palestine, from the traditional Semitic invasions, coming from the deserts in the east, such as the Israelite invasion of Biblical times and the Arab invasion of the seventh century. The Eastern invaders, infiltrating the country, speaking a similar language, looking much like the inhabitants who themselves are the descendants of former invaders, are easily absorbed into the mainstream of Palestinian culture, which has always been a melting pot of varied Semitic influences.

* * *

Like Israel, the Crusaders' state had its problems with diverse elements of the population—the European

(Frankish or Ashkenazi) ruling class; the native members of the state (the Poulains, as oriental Christians were called, or the Sephardim, as we call the oriental Jews today), and the native Muslim population left within the frontiers of the new state without really belonging to it.

Like the Israelis, the Crusaders excelled in battle, knowing that their security rested on their readiness to withstand enemy attack. Like the Kingdom of the Star of David, the Kingdom of the Cross continued to expand by warfare long after it was first established. At their height, the Crusaders' states controlled a far greater area than that conquered by Israel even in the 1967 war; it included the whole of the Syrian and Lebanese seaboard, as well as eastern Turkey and at least a foothold in the Transjordanian hills.

Much as some Israelis tend to consider themselves as establishing a beachhead for the whole Jewish people and look down upon other Jews as shirkers and deserters, the Crusaders thought of themselves as the vanguard of Christendom acting and fighting for all the Christians of the world. The deep concern of Jews everywhere for the fate of Israel during the 1967 war echoed the waves of anxiety that would awaken Europe whenever the Kingdom of Jerusalem was in danger. This relationship formed in both instances the basis of the economy. Long before the gap in the international balance of payments was invented, the Kingdom of Jerusalem was dependent upon a heavy and continuous flow of capital from Europe in the form of gifts, religious and secular grants, alms, and pilgrims' taxes. The whole of Europe became the domain of a kind of United Crusaders Appeal.

If the *kibbutzim* are a unique creation of Zionism, so

were the great military orders an authentic invention of
the Crusaders. Settlement followed a strikingly similar
pattern. A fortress manned by the Knights of the Temple or the Hospital would be established deep in Arab
territory, much like Israel's frontier *kibbutzim*, some of
which, in fact, are built around the ruins of Crusaders'
castles. Around the castle, relying on it for defense,
individual settlers would slowly create a pattern of
colonization. Some of the villages seem to have had a
kind of cooperative organization, like modern Israel's
moshavim. The military orders increasingly overshadowed the government of the kingdom. Their strength
was based upon a combination of their military potential and economic importance. In this, they resemble
some of the modern Israeli party organizations based
on *kibbutzim* and a multitude of economic enterprises,
giving them a disproportionally important voice in the
government.

One could go on making these comparisons, right
down to details. Was King Baldwin I so dissimilar to
old David Ben-Gurion? Who resembles Moshe Dayan
more than Reynald of Châtillon, the raider of Moslem
caravans, the hawk of the kingdom, the man who became so obnoxious to the Arabs that Saladin personally
saw fit to cut off his head?

* * *

In rejecting the analogy in toto, the Zionists point
out what they consider the decisive difference. The Crusaders, they believe, never were a majority in their own
states. They were but a small layer of conquerors superimposed on the native population.

This point is highly debatable. If one includes in
Crusader society the native oriental Christians, as cer-

tainly one must, the Crusaders seem to have been well in the majority. If Israel, on the other hand, annexes the newly occupied territories, Hebrew society may well find itself soon enough a minority in its own state.

Were the Crusaders a nation, rooted in Palestine in the way that the new Hebrew nation certainly is? This question must be answered in any comparison between the two. It is, of course, difficult to apply a modern term like "nation" to a time in the past in which the very notion of nationality was unknown and inconceivable. I use the term here in the sense of a community that thinks of itself as a distinctive entity, tied to a specific territory. Did the Crusaders, even those who were eighth-generation *sabras* (as we nowadays call Israeli-born Jews) consider themselves Palestinians, destined to live and die in their country, or did they think of themselves rather as Franks, Germans and Italians, serving on a foreign shore, who could go back any time to their real homeland? One rather thinks that many of those descendants of the old established Crusader families, and certainly the oriental Christians, considered Palestine, by the end of the thirteenth century, their only true homeland. But nothing like the Israeli nationality, with its fierce sense of belonging to the country—with a new and common language uniting all newcomers from many lands—seems to have evolved.

In summing up his *History of the Crusades*, Runciman records these memorable words:

Outremer (meaning "beyond the sea," as the Europeans called the Crusader states) was permanently poised on the horns of a dilemma. It was founded by a blend of religious fervor and adventurous land-hunger. But if it was to endure healthily, it could not remain dependent upon a steady supply of men and money from the West. It must justify its

existence economically. This could only be done if it came
to terms with its neighbors. If they were friendly and pros-
perous, it too would prosper. But to seek amity with the
Moslems seemed a complete betrayal of Crusader ideals;
and the Moslems for their part could never quite reconcile
themselves to the presence of an alien and intrusive state
in lands that they regarded as their own. . . . The Crusaders
made many mistakes. Their policy was often hesitant and
changeable. But they cannot be entirely blamed for failing
to solve a problem for which, in fact, there was no solution.

Yet Runciman shows that even among the Knights of
the Cross, there arose a party which favored integration
of the kingdom into the Middle East, which sought to
turn the Crusading state into a partner of the Arab
world. The same basic idea, presently being voiced by
us in Israel, seems to have much more chance of success.

The Zionists and their Israeli descendants have never
thought of themselves as having a holy mission to fight
the Arabs. On the contrary, most of them sincerely
believe that the animosity of the Arabs to their state
rests on a regrettable misunderstanding. This, of
course, is an illusion, but the very fact that such an
illusion can exist shows the basic difference. No Crusader could ever have believed that the war between the
Christians and the Moslems was anything but willed by
God. Thus, without disregarding the disturbing implica-
tions of the Crusading period for the future of Israel, no
one, neither Israeli nor Arab, should carry this analogy
too far and derive from it a fatalistic fear or hope.
Rather, this analogy should be seen as a lesson from
which useful conclusions can be drawn for the guidance
of our future actions. As one eminent historian once

told me discussing this analogy, "Israelis should view the *History of the Crusades* as a practical guidebook of how not to do it."

* * *

The Crusader Kingdom of Jerusalem seems to have doomed itself to oblivion by relying solely on its superior military organization and valor. Yet the astonishing feats of arms that carried the Crusaders into the heart of Egypt tend to obscure the real problems which determined their destiny in the long run. These same problems are valid today in an Israeli context. Without a mental readiness to become a part of the Middle East, without a policy aimed at securing acceptance by the peoples in the region, any security could only be temporary.

The Crusaders captured Jerusalem in July, 1099, celebrating the event with a terrible massacre, killing Muslims and Jews alike until they had to pick their way through corpses and blood that reached up to their knees, as a contemporary, Raymond of Aguilers, described it. The last of the Crusaders was evicted from Acre in 1291. In all these hundred and ninety-two years, despite many truces, armistices and ceasefires, the Crusaders knew not one day of real peace. In this respect, the analogy with Israel is complete.

In fact, thinking about the 1967 war, which sprang up so suddenly and unexpectedly, I am reminded of a story from the time of the Crusades which has always seemed to me the epitome of the very existence of the Kingdom of Jerusalem. In the year 1183, only four years before the armies of the kingdom were crushed by Saladin at the Horns of Hattin, a little hill overlooking the Sea of Tiberias, a marriage was celebrated in the castle of Kerak, whose ruins today overlook the Dead Sea from the east. The Lord of the castle, the notorious Reynald, Lord of Transjordan and leader of the war party, was presiding over the marriage of a seventeen-year-old nobleman to an eleven-year-old princess. From all the far-flung territories of the Crusading states, from the north of Syria to the frontiers of Egypt, the barons and noblewomen rode to the event. Some must have ridden for two weeks, carrying with them their armor, without which life was unthinkable. The celebration was in full swing when suddenly the Muslim army under Saladin materialized from the desert and fell upon the town. Before the Crusaders could rally, Saladin forced an entrance. Reynald himself was able to escape back into the castle, owing to the heroism of one of his Knights, who, single-handedly, defended the bridge over the fosse between the town and the citadel until it could be destroyed behind him.

As Runciman describes the scene:

With a fine show of bravura the wedding ceremonies were continued in the castle. While rocks were hurled at its walls, the singing and dancing went on within. The Lady Stephanie, mother of the bridegroom, herself prepared dishes from the bridal feast which she sent out to Saladin. He, in return, asked in which tower the young pair were housed and gave orders that it should not be bombarded by his siege-engines. But otherwise he did not relax his efforts. His nine great mangonels were in continuous action, and his workmen almost filled up the fosse. Messengers had hurried to Jerusalem to beg the King for help. He summoned the royal army, which he put under the command of Count Raymond; but he insisted on coming himself in his litter with his men. They hastened down past Jericho and up the road by Mount Nebo. On his approach Saladin, whose engines had made little effect on the mighty walls of the fortress, lifted the siege and on December 4 moved back toward Damascus. The King was carried in triumph into Kerak; and the wedding-guests were free to go home.

In a more modern and less chivalrous setting, this is more or less what happened during May and June, 1967, except for the fact that Reynald was not appointed Minister of Defense of the Kingdom, and he did not sally forth from the besieged fortress to attack Saladin's army and destroy its mangonels before they had time to mount the attack themselves.

This happened before and will happen again, unless Israel succeeds in gaining acceptance in the region and integrates itself into its framework. Otherwise it must be ready to fight every single day of its existence—ever prepared for all-out war, which may break out quite unexpectedly at all times, as it did in the summer of 1967.

6: David Green Comes to Jaffa

THERE WAS NOTHING extraordinary about the youngster who arrived in Jaffa one day in 1905. He was short of stature, not very handsome, yet there was a determined air about him. His name was David Green. He soon gave himself another name: Ben-Gurion.

Attlee said of himself, in comparison with Churchill, "There are men born to greatness. I am not one of them." Neither was David Green from Plonsk. But he was born to politics, and he became much more than an ordinary politician. He had the ability to completely identify himself with whatever seemed important to most people at any given time, managing to be a little bit—but not too much—ahead of them. The story of Ben-Gurion, therefore, is a mirror of Zionism. As such, it is worth contemplating, not because Ben-Gurion shaped his time, as his idolaters believe, but because his time shaped him.

* * *

Plonsk, his birthplace, is a little town not far from Warsaw. The name sounds so comical in Hebrew it has become the butt of innumerable jokes and limericks in Israel (some of which, I am immodest enough to admit, were written by me).

For a Jewish boy born in Plonsk in 1886, under czarist rule, there was a limited range of possibilities. If he was ambitious, rebellious, idealistic, he could become a Bolshevik, a Bundist or a Zionist.

The Bolsheviks believed that the great communist revolution to come would do away with anti-Semitism and pogroms. Jews should forget about being Jews as so much bourgeois nonsense. On the other hand, the Bundists (called this because they were members of the *Arbeiter-Bund,* or Workers' League in German and Yiddish) were socialists who believed that, keeping their own identity, Jews should fight as Jews for a new socialist and democratic society in their European homelands, thus solving the Jewish Question once and for all. The Zionist preached a different gospel. There was no place for the Jews anywhere but in Palestine. It was all right to be socialists—but only in their own historical homeland. Neither communism nor social-democracy would be able to do away with anti-Semitism, because anti-Semitism, according to the Zionist doctrine, was the inevitable result of the very existence of the Jews as a minority.

These three doctrines, then, were mutually exclusive, and fighting among them was bitter, made more so by the intense competition among them. Young Jews in czarist Russia were the best recruits for every revolutionary movement; if one became a Zionist, he was lost to the Bolsheviks, and vice versa. Thus the enmity that arose among these movements went far beyond mere ideological quibbling. To this day, Soviet Russia's attitude toward Israel is influenced by the ancient hatred,

imbedded in the mentality of all old-guard Bolsheviks
and their pupils. The same hatred, at times bordering
on the pathological, is just as typical of old-time Zionists. When Russia sided with the Arabs in the 1967
war, people in Israel were only confirmed in their belief
that the Soviets want to destroy Israel, a belief to which
Ben-Gurion is a life-long adherent.

The synagogue of Plonsk was an arena for all these
early fights. Zionists, Bundists, Bolsheviks and many
others gathered there from all over Russia to preach
and proselytize. Local talent joined in these jousts.
The most effective of the native speakers was the son of
Avigdor Green, a boy who started making speeches in
his early teens. Young Green was a Zionist. Why? Possibly because of a strong traditional Jewish background, which made Zionism more attractive to him
than Bolshevism; perhaps, too, because Zionism, being
the most radical remedy, appealed to his extremist
nature. Be that as it may be, for Ben-Gurion the national revolution always came first, with the social revolution a very poor second.

* * *

Zionism, for young people in Eastern Europe at the
time—a time of unrest and pogroms throughout Russia
—meant: Go east, young man. And east he went.

On a sunny Mediterranean day young Green arrived
in the Palestine seacoast town of Jaffa. It was awful. A
vivid description of this experience appears in his first
semi-official biography, *A Man and His Generation*,
written by a gushing lady admirer, Bracha Chabas. The
description is profoundly significant because it could
have come only from Ben-Gurion himself, as he remembered it many years later and told it to his biogra-

pher. It must express for many who underwent the same experience their whole attitude toward the reality of Palestine.

Here was a young man of eighteen, already a veteran of Zionist politics, who had dreamed and talked for years about Palestine, approaching its shores for the first time, seeing the outline of Jaffa with its citadel and minarets rising along the horizon. In his mind Palestine was real, yet what he pictured was not the real Palestine, but rather a Palestine of the past, present and future—all three of which bore no resemblance to what he was going to see within the next few hours. His Palestine of the future was a wonderful land of liberty, equality and Jewish resurrection, the utopia of Herzl overlaid with the dreams of eastern European socialism. His Palestine of the present was a scattered handful of isolated settlements, created since the 1880's by the pioneers of the first *aliyah*, places of heroic struggle where Jewish workers toiled and Jewish guardsmen, legendary figures, watched. The presence of half a million Arabs was only dimly perceived in this picture, a minor obstacle, much as the Samaritans were looked upon as a source of nuisance to the Jewish settlers returned from Babylonian exile under Nehemiah and Ezra some 2500 years before.

It was the Palestine of the past, of the Bible, which was most real to new arrivals like David Green; to them, the Bible was alive. In a way quite incredible to foreigners, the Bible is for Zionists, and anyone who has been to an Israeli school, a book of today—not a book of religion, literature or even ancient history, but a book of intense topical interest, a book of reference—conscious or unconscious—in dealing with the most immediate questions. Arrivals like Ben-Gurion neither

knew nor cared what had happened in Palestine since
the last Jewish rebellion under Bar-Kochba in the first
century. The victory of Islam, the Crusades, the Mon-
gol invasion, the battles of Ibrahim Pasha and various
local chieftains fighting Ottoman rule—all these, with
the ruins and edifices they left behind, seemed irrelevant, even illegal, interruptions in the history of Eretz-
Israel, the land of Israel. History, as taught today in
Israeli schools, has very little to do with all these hap-
penings. It follows the history of the Jews as seen
through Zionist eyes, leaving Palestine with the destruction of the Temple and returning with the first *aliyah*.
Ben-Gurion later took an active interest in the eradica-
tion of names connected with the in-between history,
even in foreign transcription. Thus, visitors to Israel
today see road signs in English saying "Yaffo" instead
of Jaffa, "Lod" instead of Lydda, "Tsfad" instead of
Safed, names which have been imbedded in European
consciousness since early Christian or Crusader times.

Jaffa in 1905, not yet "Yaffo," was a picturesque
oriental town. To anyone in love with the Orient it was
enchanting. The harbor accommodated only small fish-
ing boats. Passengers arriving from abroad were transferred, a few hundred yards from the shore, to small
boats, which were maneuvered perilously between the
rocks by muscular Arabs, whose lexicon consisted
mainly of juicy oaths and imprecations, in which the
Arab language happily abounds.

Was this Eretz-Israel, the land of our fathers, David
Green asked himself (as recounted by Bracha Chabas).
The scene meeting his eyes, ears and nostrils was
distasteful to the point of loathing. The smells were
evil, the guttural sounds of the Arab language an
offense to the cultured ear. The town was dirty, the

shops devoid of windowpanes, the whole place a lusty cacophony of noises. It was upsetting that there were no Jewish workers in the port. The Jews of the town, oldtimers as well as new immigrants, lived among the Arabs.

The young man from Plonsk was quite unprepared for all this. It came as a tremendous shock, and Ben-Gurion never quite recovered from it. Later in life he more or less learned several languages. He was apt to tell people that he had learned Spanish for the sole purpose of reading *Don Quixote* in the original, but he never even tried to learn Arabic, a language much more closely related to Hebrew than French or German are related to English. During his first ten years as Prime Minister of Israel, when more than ten per cent of the *voters* were Arabs, he never once visited an Arab town or village, never once received an Arab delegation. During an official visit to Upper Nazareth, a new town built by his Ministry of Defense for the express purpose of keeping in check nearby Arab Nazareth, he pointedly refrained from visiting the Arab town whose voters heavily contributed to the majority of his government in Parliament. Last year, when the Grand Old Man started a conversation with some left-wing Arab deputies in the *Knesset*, it created such a sensation that no one even pretended to listen to the unfortunate speaker of the moment, an event duly recorded by parliamentary correspondents.

So much for the first shock. Worse were to come. It took Ben-Gurion only a few days in the new country to realize that something was awfully wrong even in the small Jewish *Yishuv*. By then the original pre-Zionist settlers had been in the country for twenty years. Some had become rich plantation owners. Like the oldtimers

of the first Crusades, who had scandalized the new
Frankish knights arriving from Europe, these oldtimers
of the first *aliyah* had come to adopt many Arab habits.
They resented the new immigrants with their new-fan-
gled socialist ideas and anti-Arab attitude, their aggressive demands for employment. They much preferred
the cheap and willing Arab laborers, who did not know
what a trade union was. They despised the Hebrew
language, spoke Yiddish and had even learned some
Arabic. (An old Israeli joke describes a new immigrant
coming to the first-*aliyah* village of Metulla in the
northern tip of Palestine and asking directions in Hebrew of an old Jewish farmer working with an Arab
laborer in a garden. The farmer turns to the Arab and
asks him in Yiddish: *"Ahmed, wus sugt er?"*—meaning, "What is he saying?")

A gulf separated the new pioneers from these oldtimers and spawned a hatred never quite healed. It centered around the question that became the *leitmotiv* of
Ben-Gurion's life for many years: the question of Hebrew Labor.

* * *

Socialists who visit Israel fall, generally, into two
categories. Most become starry-eyed, overwhelmed by
our cooperatives, our *moshavim* (cooperative settlements) and *kibbutzim* (communal villages). Quite
rightly they see these as unique creations, a form of life
devoid of coercion, a state of voluntary equality seldom
achieved anywhere else. Others are disquieted by what
they see as a subjugation of socialism to nationalism.
Until only two years ago the official name of that great
institution, the *Histadruth*, was "The General Federation of Hebrew Workers in Eretz-Israel," a national-

religious definition rather than the usual territorial one. (When the word "Hebrew" was finally dropped from the name, the one man who most strenuously objected was Ben-Gurion.) Until a few years ago, the *Histadruth* did not even accept Arab members. The two sides of the Zionist socialist movement, the socialist and the nationalist, were not only interrelated, they were one and the same. The question of Hebrew Labor is an outstanding example of this, quite apart from its position as a main cause of the present situation in the Middle East. Indeed, it is no exaggeration to say that the struggle for Hebrew Labor was the real beginning of the Israeli-Arab war.

Perhaps no struggle ever started for more idealistic reasons. Zionist socialism, from the outset, was not content with transferring Jews to Israel, nor with setting up a Jewish national home. "Liberation," to have a real meaning, must also liberate the Jews from their despicable existence as shopkeepers, moneylenders and middlemen, a parasitical existence depicted in Zionist schoolbooks in a way rather reminiscent of anti-Semitic literature. No, Jews had to become workers. Professors must be turned into farmers, tailors into mechanics, merchants into carpenters, and shopkeepers into dashing guardsmen. This was the "upturning of the social pyramid," designed to give Jewish society in Eretz-Israel a broad base of workers and farmers. Together with the "religion of toil," the belief that there is something cleansing in manual labor, this was one of the fundamental aims of Zionist socialism.

It was a beautiful idea. Without it, there would be no Israel today, and certainly no *kibbutzim*. It created the revolution that made labor respectable, that demanded a technological state of mind—a revolution without which no underdeveloped country in the Middle East, or anywhere else, has any chance of joining the march of modern industrial society.

Yet this very idea created the need for employment, as well as the need for land. Hebrew Labor meant, necessarily, No Arab Labor. The "redemption of the land" often meant, necessarily, "redeeming" it from the Arab *fellahin* who happened to be living on it. A Jewish plantation owner who employed Arabs in his orange grove was a traitor to the cause, a despicable reactionary who not only deprived a Jewish worker of work, but even more important, deprived the country of a Jewish worker. **His** grove had to be picketed, the Arabs had to be evicted by force. Bloodshed, if necessary, was justified. This was the battle of Hebrew Labor, which continued for two generations, and relapses of which still trouble present-day Israel from time to time. Recently some bombs were thrown in the Yemenite quarter of Tel Aviv, to try to induce restaurant owners and bakers to fire their Arab employees.

The struggle for the redemption of the land became, at times, as violent. The land was bought, often at exorbitant prices, with good money raised mostly by poor Jews abroad. In many cases, the Arab who sold it did not live on the land, but was a rich *effendi* whiling away his life in the casinos of Beirut or the French Riviera. He had no particular care for the fate of the poor *fellahin* tenants who made their meagre living there. These were simply evicted when the land was redeemed by the Jewish National Fund in order to set up a *kibbutz*. If some of them later attacked the *kibbutz*, it only showed that an efficient system of armed defense was imperative. Thus the *Histadruth* became the sponsor and patron of the *Haganah*, the underground army based on the *kibbutzim*, which became the forerunner of today's Israel Defense Army.

Hebrew Labor, more than anything else, more than international politics, created the gulf between the two peoples living in Turkish and British Palestine. Social intercourse between them became non-existent, economic ties rare and peripheral. Long before partition was decreed by the U.N. it was a fact of life in Palestine. Jaffa and Tel Aviv, as much two parts of one city as the Bronx and Manhattan, belonged to two different worlds, with an invisible line, seldom crossed, dividing them even in times of comparative peace, until Jaffa was conquered in March 1948.

One might ask: Was this unavoidable? Couldn't Zionism have sponsored from the beginning an integrated Palestinian economy to provide labor both for Jews and Arabs? Couldn't the land have been settled by both Jewish and Arab farmers? Couldn't the *kibbutzim*, incredible as this may sound, have taken in Arab members? In short, couldn't Zionist socialism have become international, Palestinian, Semitic at its inception? These questions were indeed raised, at times, by one isolated voice or another. Dr. Arthur Rupin, one of the more far-sighted Zionist leaders and an organizer of Jewish settlements, warned in a letter in 1911 against stressing the idea of Hebrew Labor, and in another letter in 1914 proposed that a part of all land newly acquired should be set aside for the settlement of Arab tenants. But such ideas found no echo at all. The dominant sentiment was expressed by one of the elder statesmen of Zionism, the redoubtable Menachem Ussishkin, the very man who defeated Herzl on the Uganda proposal. As early as 1905, in a brochure called *Our Program*, stating that "all Eretz-Israel, or at

least the greater part of it, will be the property of the
Jewish people," he dealt with the phenomenon of Arab
employment in the Jewish economy. This, he wrote,
was a "painful leprosy."

*   *   *

Hebrew Labor, Hebrew Land and Hebrew Defense
were the three main themes of Zionist socialism
through the first half of this century. Because of them,
the socialist wing of Zionism became much more nationalistic than the bourgeois right wing, representing a
middleclass that was tainted by the long record of Arab
employment in the privately owned orange groves.
This, I believe, was the main factor enabling the Workers' Party, the *Mapai*, to become the center of power in
the Zionist movement, and later in Israel, a position it
has held without interruption since the early 1930's.

But long before then the forerunners of this party set
the tone in Jewish Palestine. They *did* things. They
represented do-it-yourself Zionism. And no one represented it more than David Ben-Gurion.

As a politician, Ben-Gurion has always had an uncanny knack for sensing where the focus of power is at
any given time, a by-no-means easy feat in the changing
scene of the Jewish *Yishuv*. Ben-Gurion was where the
power was. Following his turbulent career, you can
trace the development of the *Yishuv* from a tiny community in Turkish Palestine to the militant Israel of the
Sinai campaign and after.

According to legend, Ben-Gurion, on his arrival in
1905, became a laborer in the South Galilean village of
Sejjera, and a worker in the wine cellar of Rishon-le-
Zion. These facts have been disputed by malicious con-
temporaries, but there is no disputing his main preoc-

cupation: He was a professional party politician, who played a great, but by no means sole, or even main, part in the establishment of the political groups who later merged in the *Mapai*. These groups quickly became the main force in the *Yishuv*, thereby exerting a growing influence on Zionist politics in general. While more illustrious Zionist leaders like Weizmann and Jabotinsky stayed abroad making speeches and playing at world politics, Ben-Gurion and his associates created the instruments of action in Palestine which became inevitably the basis of power there.

Because of his Russian citizenship, Ben-Gurion was exiled by the Turks from Palestine during World War I. He went to the United States, married a nurse there, took part in the recruitment of volunteers for the Jewish battalions in the British Army (the Jewish Legion, a project for which Jabotinsky had been agitating in England) and returned with them to Palestine after the fighting there had ended. While still in the uniform of a British sergeant, he devoted his time to labor politics. The creation of the *Histadruth* was the crowning of his and his friends' endeavors. Ben-Gurion became its general secretary.

Most of the disputes of this period centered around the great debate between "practical" (do-it-yourself) Zionism versus "political" Zionism. The labor leaders, including Ben-Gurion supported by Weizmann, believed in the first course, Jabotinsky and the right wing believed in the second one. Practical Zionism meant creating bases of power in Palestine, *"dunam after dunam, goat after goat."* (A *dunam* is 1000 square meters, the basic unit in Palestinian agriculture.) Every *kibbutz*, every factory, every house is a step toward the fulfillment of an aim. What aim? The practical Zionists refused to state that the aim of Zionism was, indeed, the setting up of a Jewish state in Palestine. They thought quite rightly that this would only solidify the opposition of the Arabs. It was much better to be satisfied with talking about a national home which would bring immeasurable benefit to the Arabs. The political Zionists did not believe in all this. They did not like the *kibbutzim*, thought that practical Zionism led nowhere, that the real aim of Zionism should be to get Britain to support the idea of a Jewish state.

History has proved Ben-Gurion and his colleagues right. Jabotinsky and his Revisionist Party, so called because it wanted to revise the official Zionist line, had not much to show for their political efforts. The only real mark they made on the history of Zionism was, curiously enough, in the field of very "practical" Zionism—gun Zionism. Immediately after World War I, Jabotinsky wanted to entrust the defense of the Jewish community in Palestine, the *Yishuv*, to a new Jewish legion within the British Army. After a short experience as a lieutenant in the Jewish Battalion, he came to believe only in a regular army under British command. The practical Zionists derided this idea and created, within the labor movement, an illegal, clandestine, underground army, equipped with odds and ends of weaponry accumulated in the settlements. This organization, the *Haganah*, split several times along ideological lines, and one of its splinters eventually became, under Jabotinsky's political leadership, the *Irgun Tsevaï Leumi*, the National Military Organization that started the fight against the Arabs and the British alike. Here was "practical" Zionism with a vengeance.

Practical Zionism created the power structure of the *Yishuv*, centered on the *Histadruth*. This was the organization, becoming yearly more important, that directed the settlement of new *kibbutzim* and *moshavim*; commanded the *Haganah*; set up economic *Histadruth* enterprises and cooperatives; controlled the labor market; created the Sick Fund, which nearly monopolized medicine; and operated one part of the Jewish autonomous educational system. As the *Histadruth* general secretary, Ben-Gurion was at the very seat of power, though far from being its sole leader. Many of his colleagues in the collective leadership of the labor movement thought him much too impulsive and extreme, yet he had his hands on the practical instrument of power. Official politics, such as dealings with the British Government, he left to others, believing, quite rightly, that they were much less important than creating the cells of actual Jewish power, the state-within-the-state which was called by the Zionists themselves, "the state-on-the-way." This state-on-the-way was, of course, 100 per cent Jewish, and inevitably linked with the fight for Hebrew Labor and Hebrew Land. In this fight, Ben-Gurion distinguished himself, organizing strikes against the orange growers who dared employ Arab workers; indeed, his growing fame as a resolute fighter for Hebrew Labor was the basis for his increasing popularity. It is easy to find quotations from his speeches mentioning the need for some understanding with the Arabs, even the need for some contact with the Arab workers; Ben-Gurion has always been a prolific speaker and writer, though not a very good one, and anyone can easily find in these speeches and writings support for any point of view. But such statements are unimportant, even irrelevant, compared with his actions, and the latter indicated no place for Arabs, no plan at all for dealing with the Arab problem.

Ben-Gurion has always been a pragmatist, with a tendency to identify his own job at any particular time with the immediate, paramount need of the nation. When he was only a party politician, Jewish socialism was proclaimed by him as the only important issue. When he became the General Secretary of the *Histadruth*, immediately after the *Histadruth* was founded (Hanukka 1920) the class struggle, and the special task of the workers in building the country, became his main theme. But in the Thirties, he titled one of his books *From a Class to a Nation*, saying that the workers' class must now become the nation as such. For by then, Ben-Gurion had risen from the *Histadruth* to national office.

This came about accidentally. One night in June, 1933, a Zionist leader named Chaim Arlozoroff was murdered on the seashore at Tel Aviv, near the place where the Dan Hotel stands today. Arlozoroff was a brilliant young man who held the office of chairman of the directorate of the Jewish Agency. This, in effect, made him the prime minister of the state-on-the-way. (He was also one of the most progressive Zionists; a few weeks before his murder, he had publicly objected to the view that "what is good for [Jewish] Eretz-Israel is bad for [Arab] Palestine, and what is good for Palestine is bad for Eretz-Israel." He might have been thinking about some way of solving the Jewish-Arab problem.) The circumstances of the murder have never been cleared up. Ben-Gurion and all his friends accused followers of Jabotinsky, who were indicted but finally acquitted after a long and stormy trial. Others believed that Arlozoroff was killed by Arab criminals intent on raping his wife, and more sinister theories abound.

Whatever the truth may be, his death cleared the way for Ben-Gurion, who became the Zionist Prime Minister, a position he held until he proclaimed the independence of Israel.

Ben-Gurion assumed the national leadership at precisely the time when practical Zionism, working mainly through the workers' movement, had finished the first stage of its job. The Jewish community in Palestine now numbered nearly 300,000 people endowed with all the attributes of a real nation. Within the next few years, Hitler's regime of terror in Germany drove tens of thousands of German Jews, with their capital and know-how, to Palestine, strengthening the *Yishuv* still further. The idea of a Jewish state became feasible. Indeed, after the Arab Rebellion of 1936, a British Royal Commission, under Lord Peel, officially proposed for the first time the partition of Palestine and the setting up of a Jewish state in a part of the country.

Ben-Gurion was now the national leader and an international figure. The clash between the emergent new Hebrew nation and the British colonial regime had become inevitable. Yet Ben-Gurion was prudent. He objected to the underground war of the *Irgun*. He denounced it and even turned the *Irgun* fighters over to the tender mercies of the British police. But it was no longer a struggle over principles. Ben-Gurion, like Jabotinsky, wanted a Jewish state as quickly as possible. The only argument concerned the most efficient means of achieving it.

* * *

World War II gave the idea of a Jewish state a final and decisive push. The tragedy that befell European

Jews, which we call in Hebrew *Hashoah*, or the Holocaust, completely changed the psychological and political scene.

Throughout the war, nothing much was done by the
Zionist leadership to help the Jews in conquered Europe about to be massacred. This is still a controversial
issue in Israel, and it has not been laid to rest by the
catharsis of the Eichmann trial. Many people believe
that things should and could have been done: Hundreds
of *Haganah* and *Irgun* fighters could have been para-
chuted into Europe; the British and American governments could have been pressured into bombing the
railways leading to the death camps; the British in
Palestine could have been compelled by force of arms
to open the doors of the country to tens of thousands of
Jews who could have been rescued from Europe by
bribery and smuggling.

As a matter of fact, all the Zionist leaders, including
the two dissident underground groups, the *Irgun* and
the Stern group, conducted Palestinian, not Jewish, policies. The Jewish Agency recruited the young men of
the *Yishuv* for the Jewish Brigade in the British Army.
While they could expropriate arms for the *Haganah*,
they could do nothing about the lot of the Jews until
after the war. The *Irgun* leaders concurred in this policy until 1944, which was the year they renewed the
fight against the British.

It took some time, until nearly the end of the war,
before the news of the Holocaust finally filtered
through. (It seems to have been held up on the way by
the Zionist leadership, who did not want to aggravate
the mood of the *Yishuv*.) When its dimensions emerged
in all their horror, the news created a shock in Israel
that will last for generations.

Nothing in Israel today can be completely understood without taking into account the shadow of this genocide. It hangs over every single act and decision. It creates an outlook, a morality, a form of instinctive reaction, which can be summaried in two words: Never Again. Immediately after the end of World War II, Never Again meant that the hundreds of thousands of Jews left stranded in Europe, after the murder of nearly six million people, must be brought to Palestine immediately, into a Jewish state where these wrecks could become human beings again. Never Again meant: A state has to be set up so that never again will Jews be helpless, without the instruments of power and defense which national sovereignty confers.

For people like Ben-Gurion, it meant much more than this. The Holocaust had awakened in the whole generation of European Jews in Palestine a set of emotions long dormant. The Zionists who had come to Palestine had reacted violently to all the traditions of eastern European Jewry. They were predominantly non-religious, even anti-religious, viewing religion as an obstacle to the rejuvenation of the people. (Also, they could not forget that nearly all the leaders of Orthodox religion had denounced Herzl and Zionism, saying the setting-up of a Jewish state and the Ingathering of the Exiles were reserved exclusively to the Messiah, whose coming might well be delayed if some ungodly sinners like the Zionists took it upon themselves to do his job for Him.) Religion, then, was out. So was most Jewish literature glorifying life in the ghetto. Zionist literature, taught to every Jewish child in Palestine, depicted Jewish life in eastern Europe as despicable, the whole tradition and folk lore of the ghetto as cowardly, crooked, parasitical. (Because of this, Israeli *sabras* consider themselves vastly superior to Jews in the Diaspora, treating them at best with a paternalistic, rather colonial attitude.) Now, with the news of the Holocaust, the older Zionists in Israel, feeling guilt and repentance, found the life of their youth in the ghettos, so cruelly destroyed, beautiful, wholesome, harmonious. Jewish religion again became respectable.

All this led to an upsurge of nationalistic feeling. The state had to come, now. The dissidents intensified their guerrilla warfare against the British, sometimes collaborating with the *Haganah* and sometimes denounced and persecuted by it. The *Haganah* took over the organization of illegal immigration, started earlier by Jabotinsky, and gave it a dramatic dimension. The gallant blockade runners with their load of human misery— unfortunately Hollywoodized in *Exodus* by Leon Uris —aroused the conscience of the world. It became clear to Britain that she could not hold onto Palestine without great cost, and this did not seem worthwhile when a new British imperial strategic doctrine made Palestine seem unimportant.

When British withdrawal from Palestine in the mid-Forties became probable, the Arab problem suddenly— and for the first time—loomed large on the Zionist horizon. Ben-Gurion was one of the first to realize it. Precisely at that time, another milestone in his career was reached, again by the accident of death. After the murder of Arlozoroff, Ben-Gurion became Zionist Prime Minister. Now with the death by natural causes of Eliahu Golomb, the modest and patient founder and guiding spirit of the *Haganah*, Ben-Gurion assumed, in addition, the portfolio of Defense. Thus, just when a large-scale war with the Arabs had become inevitable, Ben-Gurion took on the job of preparing for it. The man who had struggled against the Arabs for decades in the orange groves of Petach-Tiqvah and the fields of Sejjera was now in charge of the Ministry of War.

The test of force imminent, military affairs became the focus of Israeli life. Ben-Gurion, who had never had any connection with military activity (except his short service in the British Army in World War I), overnight became the "compleat" military figure, the man in battledress, and stayed this way until the end of his office in 1963. To the new generation he became thoroughly identified as a military man. This was a far cry from the trade union leader of early days. Imagine John L. Lewis as field commander of the U.S. Army.

Both Ben-Gurion and Zionism had come a long way.

* * *

In early January, 1948, there was a secret meeting at Ben-Gurion's little house on Keren Kajemeth Boulevard in Tel Aviv. Assembled was the high command of the *Haganah* and the Jewish Agency experts for Arab affairs. One after another, the experts discounted the idea that the armies of the Arab states would interfere in the war between the Jews and the Arabs in Palestine which had broken out on November 30, 1947, the day after the General Assembly of the United Nations resolved to accept the plan for the partition of Palestine into Jewish and Arab states. Arab solidarity, the experts said, was a sham. Ben-Gurion did not believe them, and he was right. The old Arab fighter felt there would be a general Middle East war, a new round where tanks and airplanes would supersede the pistols and rifles of earlier rounds of the Zionist-Arab conflict.

By that time, the Hebrew army was already in the

field and fighting. Ben-Gurion has been widely acclaimed for creating this army, and he believes this wholeheartedly. In truth, no politician had any great part in it; the army was but a continuation of the *Haganah*, in spirit and practical outlook an authentic creation of the new Hebrew society. And yet if Ben-Gurion has rightly become an historical figure, it is because of one decisive moment. It was he who decided to proclaim, on May 14, the creation of the State of Israel, against the advice of the foreign policy experts, including Moshe Sharett, who thought that in view of American attitudes, the official proclamation should be delayed. But one should not exaggerate the importance of the proclamation as such; the Jewish state was already in being behind the front line of the Israeli Army. Every Israeli knows that neither the United Nations nor the Zionist leadership created the State of Israel, but the army, which—in an extraordinary fight—crowned the efforts of three generations of pioneers and settlers.

As the Minister of Defense, Ben-Gurion was adequate. There were many arguments between him and the dashing young military commanders, mainly on the spirit of the new army, the tradition of the underground *Haganah* clashing with the British Army tradition, in which some of the commanders had been trained. Ben-Gurion supported the British school, and, consequently, most of the successful commanders of the war resigned from the army after victory.

Another argument, more important in its consequences, concerned grand strategy. One of Ben-Gurion's deepest convictions was that on no account should Israel ever come into conflict with a Western power. This was in direct line with traditional Zionist policy, based on the conviction that in its fight with the Arabs,

Israel must have the support of one Western power at least. Thus, Ben-Gurion dragged his feet on the Jordanian front, limiting his actions against the Jordanian Army, which was commanded by British officers. Although he did much to keep the way between the bulk of Israel and Jersusalem open (even ordering a brigade into a disastrous battle at Latrun, against the advice of the General Staff), he left the Jerusalem sector command to the worst general in the army, and did nothing to conquer the Old City. Many people (including the brilliant Israel Baer, who wrote a book in prison before he died there after being convicted as a Soviet spy) believe that Ben-Gurion did not want to antagonize the British protectors of Transjordan. Indeed, throughout the war, Ben-Gurion conducted negotiations with that wily desert chief, King Abdallah of Transjordan. One may assume that from a purely military point of view, Israel could have conquered the Jordanian West Bank even in 1948.

The disputes came to a head in early 1949, when some Israeli battalions, commanded by the best general of the war, Yigal Allon, crossed the Egyptian frontier and drove to the outskirts of El Arish. From there it could easily have cut off the whole Egyptian Army in the field, captured Gaza and dictated terms to King Farouk. But at that moment the United States delivered an ultimatum. Ambassador James McDonald went to see Ben-Gurion in Tiberias, where he was vacationing, and made it clear that the U.S. would not tolerate an Israeli invasion of Egyptian territory. Faced with this threat, Ben-Gurion backed down. Allon flew up from the front to persuade Ben-Gurion not to lose this historical chance—in vain. The army was called back, and the first Armistice Agreement was signed with Egypt.

By the end of the war Israel had assumed the form
Ben-Gurion wanted. It had become a homogeneous
Jewish state, with only a small Arab minority, after
hundreds of thousands of Arabs had left the conquered
territories in circumstances to which a later chapter will
be devoted. The state was much larger, with less ridiculous frontiers than envisioned in the United Nations
Partition Plan. It was in close alliance with the United
States and in good relations with the other Western
powers. The short honeymoon with Soviet Russia,
whose vote for the Jewish state in the United Nations
had been a world-wide surprise, was drawing to a close,
but this did not particularly worry Ben-Gurion, who did
not like the Russians anyhow. In all these respects, Ben-
Gurion can be called the architect of the State of Israel,
yet in all these respects, Ben-Gurion only followed and
continued the traditional lines of Zionist policy.

He never waivered in his belief that Israel must remain a homogeneous Jewish state, that it must align
itself with the West, and that peace with the Arabs is
impossible. After the Sinai campaign of 1956, which
was his brainchild, he backed down when faced with
another American ultimatum, and again called upon
the army to retreat from Sinai. When some politicians
demanded that he at least retain the Gaza strip, he
retorted that this would be sheer lunacy, in view of the
fact that there were more than 300,000 Arab inhabitants and refugees in the Strip. An addition of so many
Arabs to the population of Israel would have changed,
in his opinion, the demographic situation in Israel, endangering its Jewishness.

The same views animated Ben-Gurion during the
1967 crisis. By now out of office, over eighty and considered eccentric by many, he objected to the Israeli

attack, believing that the Israeli Army should not be sent into battle without the direct support of at least one great power. On the morrow of the war, he first raised his voice for a typical Ben-Gurion-like demand: to raze to the ground the beautiful walls of the Old City of Jerusalem. He objected to them because they do not represent the old Israeli era, but are a reminder of the medieval Turkish phase of the history of Palestine. Fortunately, this demand did not arouse any undue enthusiasm but was viewed as a trick to attract attention to himself after a victory with which were associated the names of Eshkol, Dayan and Rabin.

After this intermezzo, Ben-Gurion had to grapple with the fundamental problem raised by the victory. He was torn between his natural desire for further expansion, inherent in the Zionist colonizing idea, and his equally strong belief that Israel must remain homogeneously Jewish. Some of his closest friends, including the poet Nathan Alterman, are conducting a rigorous campaign for the annexation of all the conquered territories in order to "liberate" what constitutes "the whole of Eretz-Israel." Ben-Gurion has not openly joined them, but neither has he repudiated the idea. Instead, Ben-Gurion is concentrating, since the Six-Day War, on two themes: increasing the Jewish birthrate and expanding Jewish immigration. Harping on these twin themes day after day, accusing his hated successor, Eshkol, of criminal negligence, he has advocated the setting-up of a new Jewish organization to stimulate the natural increase. This cannot be done by the state, he insists, because the state cannot discriminate between Jew and Arab. Only a purely Jewish body can encourage Jewish birth, without doing the same for the Arabs. On the other hand, he wants the government to deal with immigration. The Zionist organization which deals with it now is, he says, inefficient, hypocritical and useless.

Both campaigns are rather illusory. In the present stage of Hebrew society, the rate of natural increase (now 22 per 1000 yearly) will not improve significantly. Immigration has ground to a near standstill, and no real change can be expected. Even the tidal wave of enthusiasm which swept the Jewish Diaspora during and after the Six-Day War has not brought any new *aliyah* to the country.

But both hopes, unfounded as they may be, are essential to old-time Zionists, now more than ever. Only thus can they reconcile, in theory, their two natural inclinations: holding on to the conquered territories in order to colonize them, in spite of the fact that a million Arabs live there, and keeping Israel a Jewish state.

With the decision of his *Rafi* party to rejoin *Mapai* without him, Ben-Gurion has become a lonely figure on the political scene, a man without a party, without an organized following. But even today, he personifies the Zionist idea and inspires a certain kind of awe.

* * *

Ben-Gurion has traveled a long way since the day young David Green arrived in Jaffa 62 years ago. During all these years, there has not been one single day in which he was not politically active. His slogans have changed often, and so have his professed aims. He always likes to talk about the "three primary tasks of our generation." However, while the number of the tasks never changes, the tasks themselves change. What one month may be Compulsory High School Education, Conquering the Wilderness of the Negev, and Security, a month later may be Security, the Ingathering of the Exiles, and Integration of the Jewish Communities. But viewing his lifetime as a whole, one is struck by the tenacity with which Ben-Gurion followed a single straight line, from the day he was disgusted by the oriental smells and guttural sounds of Jaffa until the day he resigned from his post as Prime Minister and Minister of Defense of the Jewish state; he and Israel are deeply entrenched in the very earth of Palestine, cut off from the Arab world, but relying with complete confidence on the Israeli Army as sole guarantor of the future.

Truly, his life story is the personification of Zionism at work.

7: 1954: A Spy Story

STRANGE THINGS had been happening in Cairo in July, 1954. Bombs were exploding in cinemas and post offices, and later in the American Embassy and information offices. The Police were upset. Relations between the new regime in Egypt and the United States had been improving and were now in danger. Agents of the secret police were posted all over town.

One evening a man appeared to have caught on fire at the entrance to a Cairo cinema. Among the people who rushed to put out the flames was a secret police officer, who noticed that the flames seemed to emanate from a packet in the man's pocket. His suspicions were aroused.

This was how an extraordinary spy story came to light, an affair that was to rock Israel for many years, cause the final resignation of David Ben-Gurion nine years later and drive such men as Moshe Dayan out of the government coalition. It was also the climax of a year of fateful events, 1954, a year worth analyzing because it illustrates more than any other how the principle of the vicious circle operates in Israeli-Arab relations.

This period actually started late in 1953 with the voluntary exile of David Ben-Gurion, and ended with the massive attack of Israeli paratroopers on an Egyptian Army camp in Gaza on the last night of February, 1955.

* * *

On July 19, 1953, a small news item appeared in the papers which caused no great excitement. It said that Ben-Gurion had gone on leave, appointing Foreign Minister Moshe Sharett as Acting Prime Minister and Minister Pinchas Lavon as Acting Minister of Defense. No one dreamed that Ben-Gurion's vacation would last five months—and that afterward he would resign from the Cabinet.

Ben-Gurion himself had told friends he needed a rest in order to recharge his mental batteries and that he was joining the remote desert settlement of Sdeh Boker in the Negev to tend the sheep and meditate. This was duly and enthusiastically reported in the American press. The real reason was somewhat different. What actually happened was that Ben-Gurion suddenly found himself in a minority in his own government. He had been advocating a belligerent new line toward Egypt. The Cabinet was mainly composed of moderates led by Sharett, who overruled the Prime Minister. Ben-Gurion was really quitting in disgust, expecting to be called back very soon, after the Cabinet, without him, had made a mess of things. He was one of the many Israelis who believed Ben-Gurion was indispensable.

* * *

The chain of events that caused Ben-Gurion to advocate a more active policy toward Egypt had started a year earlier, when a group of young officers, most of them veterans of the Palestinian war, overthrew King Farouk. They were led by Egyptian General Mohammad Nagib, a quiet, pipe-smoking, middle-aged man whom Ben-Gurion seemed to have liked. In fact, Ben-Gurion publicly offered to fly to Cairo himself, to talk about peace between the two countries. This offer was, of course, ignored. No Arab politician would have dared to recognize Israel, without at least a solution to the refugee problem to clear the atmosphere. During the year, it gradually became apparent that the pleasant Nagib was only the figurehead of the Egyptian revolution. A new, quite different personality slowly emerged. This was Bikbashi (Lt. Col.) Gamal Abd-el-Nasser, a tall, handsome, entirely too dynamic young officer.

Ben-Gurion seems to have had from the beginning an ambivalent attitude toward this man, an attitude with which he infected the whole of Israel and which persists today. It is a mixture of admiration and hatred, a feeling that this man is more capable, and therefore more dangerous, than any other Arab leader. Underlying this was a deep conviction that peace was impossible because the Arabs were and would remain unwilling to make peace. This being so, any trend toward Arab unity, progress and efficiency—perhaps through Abd-el-Nasser—could only increase the threat to Israel. (Like most Israelis, Ben-Gurion was convinced that making peace was entirely up to the Arabs, and that Israel could do nothing to initiate it. Peace meant Arab recognition of the status quo, from which Israel could not and would not budge.)

Abd-el-Nasser was, in fact, the new face of Arab
nationalism, a force which no longer could be ignored
or belittled.

Another, less conscious factor may have been at
work. Ben-Gurion was nearing his seventieth birthday.
(Nasser was thirty-four.) Ben-Gurion may have felt
that something had to be done soon before he himself
became too old to lead Israel in a showdown with the
Arab world.

In any event, the first problem the new Egyptian
regime tackled was the eviction of the British Army
from its big bases in the Suez Canal Zone. (This had
been an old dream of the Egyptians. The presence of
the British Army on Egyptian soil had been a constant
reminder of the humiliation suffered by Egypt ever
since the invasion of their country by the British in the
late nineteenth century. A whole generation of young
Egyptians had grown up with the dream of throwing the
British out. While my friends and I were demonstrating
in the streets of Tel Aviv, shouting in Hebrew, "Free
Immigration—A Jewish State!" our Egyptian counter-
parts were demonstrating in Cairo and Alexandria
shouting, in English, "Evacuation!" The Egyptian Revolution broke out after a series of such demonstrations
all over Egypt, at the height of the Egyptian campaign
against the British military bases, had undermined the
Royal government in Egypt.) Abd-el-Nasser was soon
well on his way toward achieving British evacuation by
peaceful means; the Conservative government in Britain, with some American prodding, was on the verge of
concluding an agreement with the new Egyptian government providing for withdrawal.

This prospect was viewed by the Israeli government

and Army with growing misgivings. If the British left, it was felt, the Canal forever would be closed to Israeli shipping (as, indeed, it had been since the first day of the State). Egypt might be tempted to become more aggressive. Worse, the British bases were stocked with immense quantities of weapons and other military equipment, which might well fall into the hands of the Egyptians, thereby upsetting the balance of military power between Egypt and Israel.

Another disquieting thing was happening. The United States, Israel's most important ally, started to become friendly with the new Egyptian regime; the new regime, looking eminently anti-Communist, put the leaders of the three small Communist parties in prison, gladdening the heart of John Foster Dulles. A rising young star in the U.S. State Department, Henry Byroade, the Assistant Secretary for Middle Eastern Affairs, even said on July 20, 1953, that arming the Arabs was more important than arming Israel. All this was going too far. Something, obviously, had to be done before the British made a deal with the Egyptians over the bases and before the Americans became too friendly with the wrong people.

The government did not agree with Ben-Gurion on what to do, but it was entirely in agreement with him in evaluating the situation. Indeed, no one in an official position in Israel could disagree with this evaluation, based, as it was, on the main convictions common to all Zionist leaders: that the Arabs don't want peace; that Arab nationalism is an inherent threat to Israel; that the support of the Western powers is important for Israel's security; that the superiority of the Israeli Army is essential for Israel's very existence. All these convictions are elements of the vicious circle, caused by it and, in turn, affecting it.

* * *

Yet in retrospect, one wonders if the assumptions about Abd-el-Nasser were valid.

Long before Abd-el-Nasser was discovered by *Time* magazine, I was invited to have a cup of Arab coffee by a friend, Yerucham Cohen, a witty ex-*Haganah* officer of Yemenite descent. Yerucham, at the time a Hebrew University student, lived in Jerusalem in a little room on the roof of a seven-story building, without an elevator. He had called to advise me to ignore Nagib and the other young officers of the Egyptian Revolutionary Council and to concentrate on that fellow Abd-el-Nasser. "This is the man to watch," he said, "I am certain that he is the one who counts."

I asked him why. "I just happen to know him," he replied.

The full story sounds quite improbable. During the War of Liberation of 1948, Yerucham Cohen was the aide of General Yigal Allon, chief of the Israeli southern command. After we had encircled and cut off the Egyptian brigade in the so-called Faluga Pocket, Yerucham was sent under a white flag to talk with the Egyptian command. The official objective was to arrange for the burial of about a hundred of our soldiers who were killed behind the Egyptian lines during a night attack, but the real aim was to sound out the Egyptians on their possible surrender. The Egyptian commander, a huge Sudanese general known as "The Black Tiger," sent one of his younger officers, Major Abd-el-Nasser, to talk with Yerucham. The talks went on for many

weeks and a liking grew between the two enemy officers
—the one tall, the other short, but both dark-skinned
and speaking beautiful Arabic.

During one of their conversations Abd-el-Nasser
brooded that he would never see his home again, that
the whole brigade might die fighting in the Pocket.
Yerucham comforted him. "You'll see, Gamal," he
said, "you'll get back and have many children."

After the armistice the encircled brigade did get
home. Later Yerucham was appointed Israeli delegate
to the Mixed Israeli-Egyptian Armistice Commission.
From time to time he asked his Egyptian counterpart
how his friend Gamal was doing, and sent greetings.
One day the Egyptian officer told Yerucham that a
child had been born to the now Lt. Col. Abd-el-Nasser.
Remembering the conversation, Yerucham hastened to
buy a baby gift in Tel Aviv and asked the Egyptian
delegate to deliver it to his friend. At their next meeting, the Egyptian brought a message of thanks from
Abd-el-Nasser, with a big box of sweets from Gropy,
the famous Cairo café.

Abd-el-Nasser himself mentions his conversations
with Yerucham Cohen in his book, *The Philosophy of
the Revolution*, and soon after he came to power, he
did something *really* revolutionary: he unofficially invited Yerucham to meet him in Cairo. As a disciplined
Israeli citizen, Yerucham asked permission from the
Israeli Foreign Minister. The answer was no. If the
Egyptian government wants to talk to Israel, the officials said, they must talk with the Israeli government,
not with a private citizen. (Curiously, a high-ranking
West German told the Israeli government last year,
after a visit to Cairo, that Abd-el-Nasser would still like
to meet with his old friend, Yerucham Cohen.)

In light of all this, I believe that Abd-el-Nasser had no anti-Israeli sentiments or policy to start with. Coming to power quite unprepared and assuming a policy-making position without any prior plan, he seems to have had an open mind, ready to move in any direction as the opportunity presented itself or as expediency dictated, meanwhile continuing the usual verbal attack on Israel. It seems a pity that no determined effort was made at the time to see if a settlement with him could be made. But the Israeli leadership was so convinced that Arab nationalism is a threat to Israel, that the possibility of an entente with a young nationalist Arab leader must have seemed ridiculous.

* * *

To the casual observer, the situation was still tranquil, even favorable, on June 23, 1953, when Israeli and Egyptian officers signed an agreement by which each side undertook to return safely any ship and crew of the other side that might inadvertently reach its shores. On the following September 3, a Greek ship, the *S. S. Parnon*, was detained in Port Said on its way from Haifa to Elat with a load of asphalt, but several days later it was released. Israelis considered this an important step, making shipping between Haifa and Elat possible through the Suez Canal. During the Jewish High Holy Days that year, General Nagib personally went to visit the synagogue in Cairo, conveying the best wishes of the Egyptian Government to Egyptian Jewry.

But these were superficial signs; under the surface things were moving, with mounting tension. On September 17, London announced a near-agreement with Egypt on evacuation of the Suez Canal. Three days later the Israeli Ambassador in Washington, Abba

Eban, conveyed to Dulles the anxiety of the Israeli
Government about American arms shipments to Egypt.
(Dulles had visited both Israel and Egypt earlier in the
year, giving Nagib a pearl-handled pistol as a personal
gift from President Eisenhower. The U.S. Secretary of
State hoped to persuade Egypt to become the corner-
stone of a new Western-oriented military alliance of
Middle Eastern countries, a buffer against Soviet attempts to penetrate the area.) On October 5, the Egyptian Revolutionary Council met in secret session,
without Nagib, and appointed Abd-el-Nasser Prime
Minister of Egypt.

Eight days later the Israeli press published its first
item on the impending resignation of Ben-Gurion; the
same day a woman and two children wer killed in an
Israeli village. On October 15, a unit of the Israeli
Army, in retaliation, attacked the Jordanian village of
Kibieh, destroying forty houses, killing fifty people—
men, women and children. The massacre shocked the
world; it shocked the Israeli Government as well. The
blame was laid on General Moshe Dayan, then number
two man in the army. He had set up a special "Unit
101," for such retaliation raids. (Its leader was Arik
Sharon, who became one of the outstanding commanders of both the Sinai campaign and the Six-Day War.)
On December 6, Ben-Gurion resigned. His last act was
to appoint Moshe Dayan as Chief of Staff of the Israeli
Army, thus insuring that the three key offices—those of
Prime Minister, Minister of Defense and Chief of Staff
—were manned by three people—Sharett, Lavon and
Dayan—who detested each other.

* * *

Pinchas Lavon, who had suddenly become Minister of Defense, had no previous military experience. His reputation rested mainly on his brilliant polemic abilities. For years he had been considered a dove; now, overnight, he became the most hawkish of hawks, determined to out-Ben-Gurion Ben-Gurion in the apparent turbulence ahead.

In a speech on October 30, 1953, Lavon had deplored the existing Armistice Agreements, which he described as camouflage for Arab plans to destroy Israel. He added, "Israel sees itself as an integral part of the Free World. . . . The present crisis is caused by a profound change in the policy of the American administration to the detriment of Israel. We have long felt this, but now it is coming to a head." For example, Lavon quoted a "high-ranking American personality who had recently visited Israel" (John Foster Dulles) as having been "deeply shocked by the Israeli plan for the immigration of three or four million Jews to Israel in the next ten years." (Now, 15 years later, less than a million have arrived, with little prospect of large-scale immigration in the foreseeable future.)

On September 12, it became known in London that the government of Israel had transmitted several proposals to the British. The Israeli note objected to British evacuation of the Suez Canal bases without guarantees of passage through the Canal for Israeli ships and assurances that the military power balance would be maintained. Two days later, a group of Conservative back-benchers in Parliament, known as "the Suez rebels" and composed of the most reactionary colonialist elements, demanded the immediate cessation of negotiations with Egypt, using the Israeli protest as their pretext.

While the British waivered, the Americans moved forward. On April 11, 1954, Henry Byroade made a sensational speech. He said that Israel should cease its conqueror behavior and end its assumption that violence is the only policy understood by its neighbors. Two days later, Byroade announced that American aid to Israel would be cut, and American aid to Arab development plans increased.

On April 17, Nasser officially assumed the position of Egyptian Prime Minister, purging the government of pro-Nagib elements.

Throughout this period, tension increased along the Jordanian frontier. Acts of Arab terrorism had become common; Israel retaliated in massive military raids across the frontier, Lavon and Dayan concurring in this policy. Much later, Lavon was to accuse Dayan of generally exceeding orders with larger-scale raids than the government intended, while Dayan, in turn, accused Lavon of courting the army officers by ordering retaliation raids that were not strictly necessary. One Israeli yarn making the rounds in those days was that Prime Minister Sharett opened his newspaper every morning with trembling hands, for fear of what Lavon and Dayan might have concocted during the night.

In order to understand these events, one must comprehend the mood of the country. Five years after victory in the War of Liberation, peace was more distant than ever. Arab nationalism, trying to unify the Arab world and the Arab armies surrounding Israel, posed an obvious threat to the very existence of Israel. The acts of killing and sabotage perpetrated by Arab infiltrators, many of them refugees from the territory now held by Israel, created an activist mood. "Activism," as the hard line of Israel's hawks was then called, was popular, not because people were bloodthirsty, but because it seemed the only way to safeguard the security of the state.

* * *

By May, 1954, the tension in Israel had come to a head—the State seemed abandoned by its allies, confronted with a unified Arab world and a re-armed Egyptian Army; the Suez Canal finally closed, armed infiltration creating havoc along the frontiers. Trickling down to the general public from the small circle of insiders came word that intrigues were rampant at the highest policy-making level. In this climate, the latest news looked even worse than it was. On the first of May, Henry Byroade made yet another speech. Addressing the American Council for Judaism, an anti-Zionist Jewish-American minority group much hated by the Israelis, Byroade said that Israel must put an end to mass immigration, because of the fear it generated in the Arab world, and that it must repatriate a number of the Arab refugees. Byroade thought that Israel must cease being a beachhead of world Jewry and integrate itself into the Middle East. Such ideas had been voiced before in Israel—by heretics like me. But coming from an American official they sounded ominously like a pretext to drop the alliance with Israel. When it was learned that Dulles himself had cleared the speech in advance, this assumption seemed reasonable.

That same May 1 an Egyptian minister announced the arrest of Egyptian Communists, and other Egyptian officials hinted that Egypt might well join a Western military alliance after Britain's evacuation of the Suez Canal bases, negotiations for which were renewed and nearing completion.

Just about then, the world press began publishing a rumor about Israeli activist pressure, associated with Ben-Gurion, Lavon and Dayan, for an immediate preventive war against Egypt. The *London Times* printed this rumor on May 15 and C. L. Sulzberger of *The New York Times* repeated it on June 7. On May 11, during a debate in the *Knesset*, moderates and activists clashed publicly. Prime Minister Sharett criticized American policy but warned against an anti-American mood. Lavon, on the other hand, took an extreme position: "We must ration our peace declarations," he said. "The integration of Israel into the Middle East means subjugation; it means a political, territorial, moral and cultural Arabization of Israel." He added, significantly, "May the misunderstandings between us and the great Western democracies be what they are, the link between them and us will never be severed. Any other link can only be transient and utilitarian."

Non-severance of the link was not so obvious to America and Britain. On June 12, the United States threatened Israel with sanctions, officially declaring that it would stop aid to any country that would break the Armistice Agreements in the Middle East. Anyhow, Byroade declared two days later, one cannot expect aid to Israel go on forever. Later in the month, Churchill met Eisenhower and discussed American arms shipments to Egypt, Iraq and other Arab countries and the impending British withdrawal from the Suez Canal.

A preventive Israeli attack was expected any day.

But something quite different—almost fantastic—happened.

* * *

During all this time, curiously, no provocation at all had come from Egypt. Certainly, the propaganda machine cranked as usual, and Arab refugees from the Gaza Strip crossed into Israel to steal from their former lands. But the Egyptian regime was busy getting rid of the British.

One could even say that throughout this period, the Egyptian attitude toward Israel mellowed. On June 19, General Mahmoud Riad of the Egyptian Foreign Office (who was later to become foreign minister) announced that the Arabs were prepared to accept international control over the waters of the Jordan River. This would have been, for the first time, a kind of actual collaboration between the Arabs and the State of Israel. Indeed, on June 26, President Eisenhower's roving ambassador, Eric Johnston, reached an agreement with Egypt, Jordan, Syria and Lebanon about the distribution of the Jordan waters. According to the London papers this meant, in fact, the end of the Arab boycott of Israel. However, Radio Cairo announced that same day that Israel was opposed to the agreement. Actually it was Lavon and Dayan who were against it. (This point was later obscured when the Arab states turned against the Johnston plan, giving Israel another great propaganda victory.)

Behind the scenes important things were happening. Several people believed that Abd-el-Nasser was ready, finally, for a peace settlement with Israel. The Indian Ambassador in Cairo, the historian K. M. Panikar, a man who exerted a great influence at the time because

of the close relations between Jawaharlal Nehru and
Abd-el-Nasser, became an intermediary. Panikar was
also a good friend of Sharett, who later published
Panikar's book *Asia and Western Dominance* in Hebrew. (When Sharett was compelled by Ben-Gurion to
resign his post as Foreign Minister in 1956, on the eve
of the Sinai campaign, he became the head of the
Histadruth publishing house.) As Panikar himself later
told me, Abd-el-Nasser asked him to arrange for a dis-
creet meeting with Sharett. Negotiations about this
dragged on, until the events in the beginning of 1955
made a meeting impossible.

Other well-meaning people devoted themselves to the
same cause. The Maltese socialist leader (and later
Prime Minister) Dom Mintoff, started to act as a medi-
ator between Abd-el-Nasser and Sharett, but was disappointed by the Israeli attitude, as he later told Israeli
journalists. An even more resolute attempt was made
by a Socialist member of the British Parliament, Mau-
rice Orbach, who made several trips between Abd-el-
Nasser and Sharett, trying to arrange for a meeting.
Once he brought Sharett a personal letter from Abd-el-
Nasser, starting with the Arabic words, "My brother
Sharett." (Arabs use the word "brother" rather more
loosely than Europeans.) Orbach told this later to an
Israeli Ambassador, Nathan Peled, who published the
fact.

A mysterious, but seemingly high-ranking Egyptian
functionary appeared in Paris to contact Dr. Nahum
Goldmann, president of the Zionist Organization, one
of the few Zionist leaders who believed in peace between Israel and the Arab countries and was prepared
to pay a price for it. Goldmann was asked to arrange a

personal secret meeting between Abd-el-Nasser and Sharett.

It is difficult to assess whether these Egyptian peace feelers were serious or not. They may have been mere political expediency, an attempt to neutralize Israel's stand against British evacuation and American aid to Egypt. One wonders about Sharett's attitude toward them. When these facts were later published by me and others, Sharett denied them violently. Even when such evidence was produced as the statement by Orbach, and when Panikar personally confirmed the report in a conversation with me, Sharett declared that no official invitation to meet the Egyptian leader was ever extended to him "at that time." This was begging the question, because all feelers were, of course, strictly unofficial. He may have made these denials because he was less than proud of his role that year. In 1954, as Prime Minister, he had to withstand immense pressure. His Minister of Defense withheld vital information from him; his Chief of Staff was out of control; public opinion was manipulated by the activists; and back in the shadow lurked the grand figure of Ben-Gurion, officially a hermit in the Negev but actually very active in undermining the position of his successor. Any kind of concession to the Arabs might have destroyed Sharett's political standing at the time. Only much later, stricken with cancer and aware that his end was near, Sharett— this unassuming yet proud man—had the courage to stand up to Ben-Gurion, castigating him during the later stages of the Lavon Affair in a series of speeches which gained him admiration and respect.

Arabs always believed Sharett was the opposite of Ben-Gurion. Indeed, Sharett, who had come to Palestine at an earlier age than Ben-Gurion and grown up in

an Arab neighborhood, knew Arabic well and loved
Arabic culture. He also had some of the physical features of an Arab, as well as a sense of dignity and
decorum which made him liked by the Arabs. However,
it is wrong to assume that fundamentally Sharett's attitude was different from Ben-Gurion's. The many differences of opinion between the two men concerned only
nuances and methods, Sharett generally preferring the
soft word and well-formed phrase to Ben-Gurion's
bluster.

Sharett was a man of peace. But peace for him
meant an Arab acceptance of the status quo created by
the victory of Israeli arms, including the refugee problem. It is highly significant that throughout his eight
years as Israel's first Foreign Minister, he never set up a
serious department for Arabic affairs in his ministry,
which was responsible for them.

Sharett's part in the events that follow is not quite
clear. Yet like the other Israeli leaders, he automatically discounted the possibility of an alliance with the
Egyptian regime aimed at getting the British out of the
Middle East. More than anyone else, as Foreign Minister and as Prime Minister, he believed in the absolute
necessity of Israel's alliance with the West—even if this
meant the loss of another historic opportunity to integrate Israel into the general pattern of Middle Eastern
nationalism.

Sharett must have agreed that something must be
done to sabotage the burgeoning Arab-American rap-
prochement.

* * *

In the beginning of July, 1954, a man in a Cairo
hotel turned on his radio and listened to a soft voice

coming from Israel. What he heard was a code word ordering him to set in motion the plan he had brought with him to Egypt.

It concerned a small group of young Jewish Egyptians, recruited some time before by an Israeli intelligence officer who called himself John Darling. It was an efficient spy ring, well trained, one of the many which operate in all Middle Eastern countries and form an integral part of the omnipresent military preparedness.

What the group was now ordered to do was something quite unlike ordinary espionage. The idea was to plant bombs in American and British offices throughout Egypt, thereby creating tension between Egypt and the two Western countries. This tension was supposed to enable the Suez rebels in the British Parliament to prevent an agreement providing for the evacuation of the Suez bases, and also provide ammunition for those parts of American public opinion that opposed arming Egypt. It would also create a general state of confusion and disprove the thesis that the Egyptian regime was a stable and solid base for Western policy.

The first few attempts were successful. But the members of the group, inexperienced in this special activity, could not really carry such a plan through. They also had misgivings; they loved Israel and risked their lives for it, but they were not anti-Egyptian and did not like to endanger the lives of Egyptian people. When the young man was accidentally captured at the Cairo cinema—betrayed by his homemade, premature incendiary—the whole ring broke up. Under questioning, perhaps helped by torture, some facts quickly came to light.

The man who had brought the orders escaped in

time; the other members were captured. One committed suicide in his cell, two were hanged and the others condemned to long stretches in prison. A beautiful girl—Marcel Ninio, a well-known figure in the more elegant sport clubs of Cairo—attracted special attention for her role in the group. After the Six-Day War, Israel did secure her release from Egyptian prison as a condition of the return of the 5,500 Egyptian prisoners of war captured during the war.

(One man connected with this ring who was not caught at the time was a young Egyptian Jew named Elli Cohen. A few years later, he succeeded in infiltrating the highest circles of the Syrian government, posing as a Syrian emigré living in Argentina. His astonishing success provided the Israeli Army with information which proved essential during the recent war. But long before this war, Elli Cohen had been caught and publicly hanged in a square in Damascus.)

*   *   *

The first inkling that something bad had happened in Egypt appeared in the Hebrew press on July 25. A small news item read: "According to Radio Damascus, six Zionists were arrested in Egypt. They were accused by the Egyptian police of trying to sabotage the Anglo-Egyptian negotiations. The arrested men were indicted for setting fire to the American Information Offices in Cairo and Alexandria."

The man who was the most upset upon reading this —or so he said—was Defense Minister Lavon. He did not remember ever having given the order to do this. In fact, the question, "Who gave the order?" has haunted Israel ever since, toppling governments, splitting parties and turning David Ben-Gurion into Public Nuisance

No. 1. The Egyptian aspect of the affair is generally alluded to in Israel as "The Security Mishap." Its sequel in Israel is called "The Lavon Affair." It aroused passions such as no other affair in Israeli public life, before or since, ever did.

What seems odd is that, in the consequent discussions which have been going on all these years, no one has ever really questioned the wisdom of the general line which inspired the mishap and other activities at the time, namely the wish to support the continuation of the British occupation of the Canal Zone, even at the price of further alienating—perhaps forever—the Egyptian people. The whole discussion centers around the one point: Who was responsible for an operation which, having failed, looks stupid? Other questions: Did or didn't the Minister of Defense tell the director of military intelligence to start the operation, in a private meeting with no witnesses, in the middle of July? Did the director lie when he said so, or did the Minister lie when he denied it? Were documents intentionally falsified? Were vital pieces of evidence spirited away? Were the officers responsible shielded by superior officers and the Chief of Staff himself? Were witnesses induced to perjure themselves, and why did General Dayan see fit to receive one of them just before the witness gave evidence? General Dayan, in fact, was conveniently away when the mishap happened. He was visiting the United States, causing some consternation in Pentagon circles. Dayan seems to have thought that he had been invited by the U.S. Army, while the Pentagon did not recall any such invitation; in any event, he was allowed to visit army installations at his own expense. It has never been made clear why Dayan insisted upon being in the United States exactly when things were happening in Egypt which might have had some bearing on Israeli-American relations (and about which the last one to know would certainly be the Israeli Ambassador in Washington, Abba Eban).

The failure of the operation destroyed Lavon. He was compelled to resign, and the government turned in despair to Ben-Gurion, begging him to reassume the post of Minister of Defense. Lavon himself and many others are convinced, to this day, that the whole intrigue was concocted to provide Ben-Gurion with a face-saving way to return from Sdeh Boker, where he had been waiting, with growing impatience, for his people to call him back.

The later convulsions of the affair are important only in the context of Israeli home politics. Several secret commissions of inquiry went into the matter, with varying results, until finally a "Committee of Seven" Cabinet members cleared Lavon of any responsibility. This upset Ben-Gurion so much that he resigned, making new elections necessary. Returned to office, he resigned again in 1963, under the impression that his colleagues in the government were conspiring against him. When his demand for establishing yet another commission of inquiry (in order to quash the findings of the Committee of Seven) was rejected by the government of Levi Eshkol, Ben-Gurion split the *Mapai* party, which he had helped to found, and set up his own—a rather unsuccessful one which has just now returned to *Mapai*, without Ben-Gurion. Ben-Gurion's preoccupation with this affair has by now assumed the proportions of an obsession, embarrassing and irritating even such former protégés as Moshe Dayan.

I find it highly significant that the biggest affair ever to rock the country was directly connected with the two main problems of Zionist history: relations with the Arab world and relations with the Western powers. (One should also add that the Lavon Affair had a salutary effect in certain areas, highlighting as it did some questionable practices. The Israeli Army has since become by far less involved in politics, and the secret services have been brought under more direct control.)

* * *

On July 27, 1954, the British-Egyptian Agreement was finally signed. When Israel sent a ship under its own flag, the Bat-Galim (Daughter of the Waves), to the Canal as a test, the crew was arrested and returned only after some torture and long negotiations. The ship itself was impounded.

But a much more important event ultimately drew attention away from the Canal. In the middle of February, 1955, Ben-Gurion returned to the Ministry of Defense (leaving Sharett, for the time being, as Prime Minister, in name if not in substance). Two weeks later, the Israeli Army attacked the Gaza camps, killing scores of Egyptian soldiers. This event is now considered the turning point in Middle Eastern history. Abdel-Nasser has declared many times that he decided to buy Soviet bloc arms (thereby allowing for the first time full-scale Soviet penetration into the Middle East) because of this attack, which revealed the helplessness of his Egyptian Army. There is no doubt that, with this raid, there began the period of raids and counter-raids, and ever-mounting terrorism and retaliation, culminating in the murderous campaign of the *Fedayeen*, and leading right up to the Sinai War of October 1956.

Why was this attack made? There seems to be no

clear answer. The acts of infiltration which preceded it, severe as they were, were not unusual and certainly did not deserve a massive counterstroke which upset the whole equilibrium of the Middle East. Cynics said that it was a way for Ben-Gurion to show that the Old Man was back again; others believe that Dayan was reasserting his independence and exceeding his orders as usual.

But the Gaza attack was much more significant than that. It was, in fact, a declaration of war against Abd-el-Nasser and his whole brand of nationalism, and so it was understood by Abd-el-Nasser himself. It seems the Egyptian dictator, an old hand at conspiracy and a great fan of undercover operations, was not too upset by the sabotage activities of the spy ring in Cairo, but the attack on Gaza was something else.

Just before it, two new trends had emerged that completely changed the situation of Israel. Egypt had decided not to join the Western military alliance, perhaps because it thought it did not need American assistance after the British evacuation had been assured; perhaps because it was influenced by the Afro-Asian overtures of Nehru; perhaps because the proposed pact favored Iraq, the traditional competitor of Egypt. Dulles was upset and reacted violently. All the nice speeches of Henry Byroade were forgotten, as were the anxieties about the Suez Canal bases. Washington forged ahead and created the Baghdad Pact, arming Egypt's enemies in the Arab world. Abd-el-Nasser became a Neutralist, then a dirty word in Washingtonese. The danger of an American-Egyptian *entente* disappeared, and Ben-Gurion may have thought it propitious to teach the Egyptians a lesson.

Even more important was an event which opened

completely new vistas. On October 1, 1954, the Algerian War of Liberation had begun. After losing Indo-China, Morocco and Tunisia, the French diehards were determined to fight for Algeria, "an integral part of France." Unable to understand the mechanism of modern nationalism or to reconcile themselves to facts that spelled their doom in Africa, the French naïvely believed the Algerian Revolution was nothing but a *manoeuvre* engineered by that sinister man in Cairo. They became obsessed with the idea that Nasser must be toppled; any enemy of Nasser thus became, automatically, a friend of France. Contacts were established immediately, and the attack on Gaza was certainly a good way to remind Paris where the second front could be.

The burgeoning friendship between Paris and Jerusalem, which soon became a full-fledged political and military alliance, followed the by-now traditional pattern of the vicious circle. To the Arabs, France was the most obnoxious of colonial tyrants, massacring a whole people in the vain attempt to hold Algeria. To Israel, France thus became the ideal supplier of fighter planes and tanks which Israel now desperately needed to hold its own against the vast stockpiles of Soviet arms building up in the Sinai Peninsula. Threatening the Arabs and diverting Arab aid from the Algerian liberation fighters, Israel could get any quantity of French arms needed. Yet, aligning itself with the French policy of repression, Israel incurred even greater Arab hatred, and, consequently, the need for bigger, better and more arms.

In vain did some of us in Israel argue that Israel should risk following the opposite policy. The Algerian rebels were eager to receive help from Israel, as they

would have been from any other state. Friendship with
them could have been established in their hour of need,
and when they achieved their freedom, as inevitably
they must, we would be for the first time in close contact with a least one important Arab state. For the
future security of Israel, this was more important than
Mystère fighter planes. These arguments, running
against the accumulated experience of two Zionist generations, did not gain much ground in Israel. The Israel
Committee for Algerian Liberation, which we created,
established good contacts with the F.L.N., but carried
no weight whatsoever in Israel. Today's tanks, meeting
today's dangers, are always more real than the political
outlook of tomorrow.

By the end of 1954, the road which led to the Sinai
War of 1956, to the failure of France in Algeria and,
thereby, to the end of the French-Israeli alliance, could
be clearly foreseen. (When de Gaulle made his violently anti-Israeli remarks at his press conference at the
end of 1967, we could quote hundreds of our statements during the intervening years forecasting this inevitable turn-about.) It could also have been predicted
that the future leaders of Algeria—Houari Boumé-
dienne, for one—would become the most extreme anti-
Israel element in the Arab camp.

The avenues open in 1954 were either unseen or
ignored, while Israeli policy went along the well-trod
road of traditional Zionist conviction. That year was a
crucial one—not because it was a turning point, but
rather because it was *not*.

8: Moshe Dayan: Lone Wolf

THE MAN who played an ever-growing role in 1954, was directly responsible for the attack on Gaza and the following retaliation raids, led the army in the Sinai War, and emerged again on the eve of the recent war—after some years of comparative obscurity—is Moshe Dayan. It is worth studying the life and career of Dayan, not only because of his influence in Israeli politics, but even more because Dayan himself is a perfect product of Zionist history.

Dayan is a *sabra*, a native Palestinian, so called because, like the prickly pear, native Israelis are supposed to be thorny on the outside, sweet inside. Another legend has it that *sabras* are simple-minded, upright people, devoid of complexes; Dayan is usually considered just such a man. Nothing could be further from the truth—a more complicated personality can hardly be imagined. Moshe is a man of many contradictions.

His chief trademark, the black eyepatch which makes him easily recognizable, is in itself a symbol of contradiction. The black patch is a public relations

man's dream. (American publicity experts, who used
the black patch for a well-known and immensely successful advertising campaign for a brand of shirts,
chose it because it automatically attracts attention.) In
many newsreels of the June war, you saw a large group
of officers entering the Lion's Gate of ancient Jerusalem, and you immediately and unconsciously focused
on the black patch of the man in the middle. In the
summer of 1967, whether his picture hung in a lower
Manhattan shop window or appeared on the cover of a
magazine in West Berlin, everyone knew the patch and
its owner. (Ben-Gurion's shock of white hair, Castro's
beard set them apart in the same way.) Yet Dayan is
not happy with the patch.

He has every right to be proud of it, reflecting as it
does his long service to the nation. He was wounded in
1941, when he acted as a liaison officer with the Australian forces advancing into Lebanon during the campaign of the British and the Free French to evict the
Vichy regime from Syria. Dayan and some other *Haganah* members were with an advance unit of the Australian Army which captured bridges and outposts
along the way. After taking a police building, Dayan
went to the roof and looked through his binoculars,
with typical nonchalance, at the enemy still surrounding
the building. A French sniper hit the binoculars, which
smashed into his left eyesocket and stuck there. A com-
rade tried to remove them but only made the wound
worse; throughout, Dayan never lost consciousness. For
years later, Dayan consulted world-famous specialists,
who tried to fit him with an artificial eye, but because of
the wound in the socket, this was impossible. Dayan
still suffers a great deal from this injury: When he
wears the patch, the warm air behind it presses on the

wound, causing him irritation and pain. As a result, he does not wear it at home or in the office—and suffers the instinctive reaction of visitors who see him without it.

Thus, his eyepatch is a source of conflict for Dayan. He knows very well that the patch is of great publicity value to him, and he takes advantage of this unhesitatingly. Nonetheless, he is sensitive about it, longs for the moment he can take it off and, therefore, hates meetings, conferences, lectures—any contact with people which compels him to put it on. When a magazine once printed a cover portrait of Dayan emphasizing the left side of his face, he took it as an insult, yet there is not one politician in the country who does not envy his trademark.

There are other physical paradoxes. In Israel, Dayan is considered a symbol of youth. Many people were astonished to hear that he is a grandfather who celebrated his fifty-second birthday three days before he became Minister of Defense in May, 1967. His face is young, almost mischievous, and does not seem to belong to his plump, nearly shapeless body—the body of a middle-aged farmer, with a farmer's lumbering walk. During the past few years, his hair has thinned, but his youthful smile makes one forget the fact. Yet the smile is devoid of any warmth; there is nothing glad in it. It is an unmoving smile, fixed on his face throughout all public appearances.

* * *

These outward contradictions reflect inner ones. The main characteristic which made Dayan a national hero during the days of anxiety preceding the recent war is his ability to make decisions without reluctance or procrastination. The public wanted him because he seemed to be the opposite of Eshkol, who (according to one current joke) when asked by a waiter whether he wanted coffee or tea, hesitated, then answered, "Half and half." The real Dayan is unlike his public image. He does decide quickly, but often the next day, another quick decision contradicts yesterday's. His decisions form a mosaic of indecision, a systemless pattern perhaps worse than simple procrastination. During the last few months, people have become accustomed to the pattern. Dayan objected to the military assault on the old city of Jerusalem, but, when overruled by the government, was the first to be photographed at the Wailing Wall. Immediately after the war, he ordered the destruction of the town of Kalkiliah and the eviction of its inhabitants to Transjordan, but a week later, in person, he welcomed the same inhabitants back to what was left of the town. During the weeks following the war, his many political statements about the future of the occupied territories, each exactly contradicting the one before, became a source of irritation even to his admirers.

Another characteristic endearing him to the public is his apparent tendency to talk straight from the heart, to tell people exactly what he thinks, without tactful embellishment. This is a soldierly trait, and indeed Dayan is terse and reasonable in his speech, detests exaggeration, always gets to the point in the shortest possible time. Unfortunately, this has nothing at all to do with sincerity. Moshe Dayan just never says what he really thinks. He neither tells the truth nor lies. Truth and falsehood are quite irrelevant in his words, which are not intended to reflect any reality, objective or subjective. Dayan uses words as any other weapon, in order to achieve, at any given moment, what he wants to achieve.

Old Zionist leaders, brought up in a different tradition, are upset by this trait. After the war, the old *Mapam* leader Meir Yaari publicly accused Dayan of misleading him. He said his party would never have agreed to Dayan's inclusion in the government if Dayan had not convinced him he was opposed to any offensive action against the Arabs. Of course, there was no connection whatsoever between such a statement, probably made by Dayan in his usual straightforward tone, and what he really thought. He certainly did not intend to become Defense Minister in order to hold parades, but if he had to assure Meir Yaari of his peacefulness in order to capture this central seat of power, the Ministry of Defense, such assurance was forthcoming. He wouldn't have dreamed of telling Meir Yaari his genuine thinking—any more than he would have told Abdel-Nasser himself. Of course, politicians throughout the world are used to using words to hide their thoughts, but generally there is a system to it. With Dayan, it is quite a different phenomenon—a deeper urge to hide whatever he thinks, whether such deception is necessary or not.

This trait, the lack of any respect for words is the result of another more profound characteristic, which may be the key to his whole personality: complete lack of communication with his fellow man. This is the source of both his strength and his weakness, his greatest advantage as well as his main limitation, the quality which makes him a superman in the eyes of his admirers, and a thoroughly disturbed personality in the eyes of his opponents.

Dayan has no contact with people. He has no close

relationship, neither in his family circle nor within a social group. He hasn't a friend in the world. He has immense charm and can entice everyone, but he cannot relate to anyone. Even his daughter Yael notes, in writing of him, "When he is in a good mood, he is very charming, but he doesn't have enough patience to persevere until he gets results." Yael adds, in a woman's magazine article meant to glorify her father, "Most people bore him. Some of them immediately, others after half an hour." Psychologists might find this a serious symptom, an inability to become interested in other human beings. Many people are ready to see Dayan's open disdain of others as a sign of greatness. Throughout history, leaders often created around them an atmosphere of aloofness, on the assumption that familiarity breeds contempt. But Dayan's contempt for people is of such magnitude that it is a deterrent to the fulfillment of his ambitions; some of his most ardent followers became his enemies when he sacrificed them, without a second thought, for the sake of expediency.

He has never had around him an entourage, a crew of advisers and confidants. In truth, he heeds no advice, and certainly confides in no one, not because he is suspicious by nature, but because he respects no one and doesn't even try to mask his contempt. It is quite usual to see Dayan stand in one of the *Knesset* lobbies, a national leader talking to him as Dayan glances about with the utmost impatience, as if saying, "Stop it! You are talking nonsense!" He never sits in the *Knesset* hall for more than a quarter of an hour at a time, always impatiently, getting up in the middle of a speech, even by one of his associates—David Ben-Gurion or Shimon Peres—with a gesture that says, "How can one listen to this?" Thus it is impossible for Dayan to be a real party

leader. When Ben-Gurion broke away from *Mapai*, on
the eve of the 1965 elections, and formed the *Rafi*
party, Dayan joined at the very last moment, just hours
before the deadline for submitting the names of the
candidates. Since then, he has seldom attended party
meetings or even visited his office at party headquarters.

* * *

What produced such a man? What makes him tick?
The answer, as close as one can come to it, is a mixture
of psychology and Zionist history.

The key may lie in some sentences written, rather
innocently, by his daughter Yael: "He is a lonely man
who consciously and intentionally chose to be lonely.
He himself holds the key to his own prison. Nevertheless, there are chinks in his armor. I believe that he was
deeply attached to his mother, my Grandma Devora,
even if he was sometimes as impatient toward her as
toward anyone else. He did not weep when she died.
..." Without doubt. Dayan was very close to his mother
in childhood, an attachment which may have determined his whole character. He did not have a similarly
close relationship with his father, Shmuel Dayan, whom
he displaced in the *Knesset*. When his father recently
remarried, Moshe became even more distant toward
him.

The boy Moshe, who grew up in the co-operative
village Nahalal in the shadow of his mother, was gentle
and sensitive. Pictures taken when he was three show
him with a sweet, round face, his left eye a bit smaller
than the right, a hereditary trait of the Dayan family. It
is the face of a boy who later would have become, in a
different society, a sentimental man, perhaps an actor,

perhaps a poet. (Indeed, until a very late age, he wrote poems, not very good ones, but not very bad either.) After primary school, he went to the agricultural high school. This is rather odd in itself, because it was a school for girls, and Moshe Dayan was the only boy there. All the other boys of the neighborhood, including some of the later generals of the Israeli Army, went to the *Kadoori* school near the hill Tabor. It is unusual for an adolescent boy to agree to attend a girls' school, even if it is more convenient.

Sometime at that age, the boy Moshe underwent his great change. Nahalal of the Thirties was not a place where artists, or sensitive children, were appreciated. It was the first co-operative settlement, a center of the settlers' movement, a place where boys showed off their manliness, chided gentle children, adored tough fighters, and dreamed of the day when they, in their turn, would till the soil and fight the Arabs. Somewhere along the way, by conscious effort, the boy Moshe decided to emulate them. Like all sensitive children who turn away from their real character, he went all the way to the other extreme, and he had to pay a price for his artificial toughening; he developed an ulcer, a psychogenic disease commonly associated with people who try to put up a false front in order to disguise their feelings. Dayan did not learn to live with his emotions, but instead, choking them, became incapable of emotional relationships with others. He is not a man who overcame fear, but rather one who killed his fears, for whom fearlessness became a cult—the warrior who runs into battle, the general who personally takes part in retaliation raids, the Chief of Staff who appears in the middle of battles during the Sinai War, the Minister of Defense who goes up in an open jeep to the Mount of Olives while snipers are firing all around. His opponents think these are publicity stunts. But basically they are the acts of a man who wants to prove something to himself all the time. Daughter Yael senses this. She tries to depict such a man in her novel, *Envy the Frightened.* The hero is always trying to demonstrate to himself that he is a he-man, thereby becoming an emotional cripple. Such cultish manliness is typical of boys of sixteen or seventeen and usually disappears later on. But Dayan, once he decided to become tough at that age, stayed that way. This may be the explanation for the public image of eternal youth, an image which had not changed by the time he was fifty-two, and which will not disappear until he dies. (A few months ago I picked up a young soldier who was hitchhiking to his base. On the way we argued about Dayan. And when I mentioned that the General was fifty-two years old, the soldier was so shocked he offered to bet his monthly salary that Dayan was not over thirty-five.)

There is something strikingly adolescent about everything Dayan does. He personally taught his three children, including the girl, how to handle a rifle, a skill hardly necessary for the pampered children of Zahala, a fashionable Tel Aviv suburb. He encouraged his older son to join the Naval Commandos and his younger son to become a paratrooper. Although he never devoted much other time to his children, he managed to take them, while they were quite small, on long desert treks. He is famous in the country for several typical exploits. Once, when he found the shortest way to his home blocked by barrels the traffic police had put up, he simply got out of his car, in a full general's uniform, removed the barrels and went on. An amateur archeologist, like many Israelis, Dayan used to break the Israeli law which forbids people to remove archeological objects, and not only occasionally, like other amateurs. During the Sinai War, when an archeological site was discovered by an advancing army unit, he had the military police close off the whole area until he had time to dig and remove some finds. His home in Zahala is well-stocked with ancient columns and jugs, each a reminder of law-breaking, a fact which does not prevent the Minister of Defense from having official receptions there between digs. "Like a child, he is proud of the negative publicity he gets as an *enfant terrible*," Yael Dayan has written.

When quite young, Dayan married Ruth Schwartz—the daughter of a well-established Jerusalem lawyer. She was a classmate of his in the Nahalal school. But there never has been a real Dayan family. The house in Zahala, so often photographed lately for the American press, is more like a federation of rooms than a family house. Before Moshe's children married, each of the family members lived in his own room, coming and going as he wanted, conducting his own affairs, rarely meeting the others at regular times; only the elderly maid, who became the center of the family, created a kind of contact among them. One of the Dayan boys used to lock his room when he went out.

If Dayan has never had a family life, hero-worshippers may see this as a sign of the superman. As his daughter sees it, "he put himself at the disposal of the nation. . . . Even though he is not a model father, there is no doubt that he gave us the strength and the wisdom to understand that this is a small price to pay for his service to the country." Thus, the image of the hero: the man who holds small things in contempt, neither smokes nor drinks, always dresses in shapeless clothes, doesn't know what good food is, sacrifices his private life for the common good, once telling his daughter, "If I had to live my life again, I would not have had a family." A psychologist might explain this behavior differently: The eternal adolescent, too much attached to his mother, who cut himself off from all contact with people and suppressed all his emotions, is also unable to lead an ordinary family life. Indeed, all his contacts with people, men and women, are hit-and-run encounters, perhaps a momentary longing for some human relating, and an immediate escape therefrom.

* * *

In Israel, as in any other country, there are many people who aspire to political power. Young politicians often distinguish themselves by an ardent desire to reach the top as quickly as possible. At least half a dozen talented young men—ex-General Yigal Allon, ex-Chief of Staff Professor Yigael Yadin, Ben-Gurion's protégé Shimon Peres, Foreign Minister Abba Eban, among others—all would like to become prime minister soon. But for no one has this ambition become so much a central theme in his life as it has for Dayan. Therein lies his great strength; no one becomes a supreme leader unless he is prepared to sacrifice everything, all other interests, to this one goal. A man interested in many things, with an open mind and intellectual curiosity, would find it hard to compete with one who single-mindedly concentrates on the attainment of power.

The man who first realized this about Dayan, was his old mentor, Gen. Yitzhak Sadeh, the legendary commander of the *Palmach*, the underground *Haganah* commando, the man who nurtured most of the outstanding commanders of the Israeli Army. A short time before he died he told me, "This is the most dangerous man in Israel. One has to watch him constantly. He has no scruples, no inhibitions, no morals. He is capable of anything." To make his point, Sadeh told me a hypothetical story: "Some day Ben-Gurion will assemble all the commanders of the army and tell them that Yitzhak Sadeh has to be arrested. He will ask for a volunteer. One after another, all the generals will back out on one pretext or another. Only one will agree to do it. That will be Moshe Dayan." After a minute's thought, Sadeh added, "And if Dayan has to be arrested, I'll do it."

Has Dayan any set ideology? The answer seems to be in the negative. Yet no man, and certainly no one in political life, is really devoid of an ideological outlook, even if an unconscious one.

Dayan is a non-intellectual, if not an anti-intellectual. Rarely does he read a book; his education is minimal and narrow. His speeches and articles, always to the point, are shallow, without depth of thinking or width of perspective; while interesting, they are not impressive, and seldom open new vistas. He has only contempt for thinkers, viewing abstract thought as a sign of weakness. Once, when accused of doing things without thinking, he retorted that it was a lot better than talking without doing. Even his one hobby, archeological digging, is not an intellectual one, but the pastime of a lonely being who goes out to dig, always alone for many long hours, and who later, at home, spends many more hours putting the pieces together, again alone. Archeology certainly is a highly intellectual occupation when it deals with re-creating a picture of history, but not when it deals only with the actual digging, hunting for objects.

A man uninterested in ideas and scornful of advisers

who might produce them, cannot stick to a set of ideas —one reason for the zigzag course Dayan always seems to follow. Having no organized group of counselors and aides, and no solid structure of thought, Dayan is unable to form a party of his own. Thus his only way to success leads through the existing major party, which he will have to take over if he is to be prime minister, even at the price of accepting an existing party machine which he detests and which may well thwart his actions. (In Israel, which has no two-party system, it would be more natural for a charismatic leader like Dayan to create his own party as an instrument for the realization of his aims. This is what Ben-Gurion did—several times.)

But Dayan, nevertheless, is guided by a central theme. With all his meandering, he always comes back to one basic line; the public senses it and, therefore, the cry went out to have him in the Defense Ministry on the eve of the recent war. Dayan was, is, and will always be an Arab-fighter. He is the Israeli equivalent of what Americans used to call an Indian-fighter, a type common in the second generation of settlers in a country where newcomers are forced to fight the native population.

If one looks through all the thousands of speeches, articles and declarations of Moshe Dayan, one finds a single speech that really expresses what he thinks. This is the eulogy he delivered at the funeral of Roy Rotenberg. Roy, a member of the *kibbutz* Nahal-Oz, opposite Gaza, was killed a few months before the Sinai War by Arab infiltrators who tried to harvest some grain. (He rode up on his horse to scare them off and was shot.) Dayan, who seems to have been uncharacteristically deeply moved, made a short speech, reading, again uncharacteristically, from a prepared text. This is the credo of Dayan who that very day had become forty-one years old:

Let us not today fling accusations at the murderers. Who are we that we should argue against their hatred?

For eight years now, they sit in their refugee camps in Gaza, and before their very eyes, we turn into our homestead the land and the villages in which they and their forefathers have lived.

. . . We are a generation of settlers, and without the steel helmet and the cannon we cannot plant a tree and build a house.

Let us not shrink back when we see the hatred fermenting and filling the lives of hundreds of thousands of Arabs, who sit all around us. Let us not avert our eyes, so that our hand shall not slip.

This is the fate of our generation, the choice of our life—to be prepared and armed, strong and tough—or otherwise, the sword will slip from our fist, and our life will be snuffed out.

This is a stark philosophy, the philosophy of a crusader who sees no doors open leading toward peace, who believes that the very thought of peace is demoralizing. On the eve of the Six-Day War, *Kol Israel*, the Israeli radio, rebroadcast this speech. It was the anniversary of Roy's death—and Dayan's birthday.

*   *   *

Dayan's is the philosophy of a man who was born in war, who has lived all his life in war, for whom war has always been the focus of thought. All the personal history of Moshe Dayan is intertwined with the Hebrew-Arab struggle.

He was born in 1915, during World War I. His parents, both immigrants from the Ukraine, met in Degania A, the first *kibbutz* in Palestine, and married against the decision of the *kibbutz*. (At the time it was still believed that marriage and child-bearing, like everything else, were proper subjects for communal decision; this orthodox attitude has since been modified.) When Moshe, the son of Shmuel and Devora Kitaigrodsky, was born, the situation between *kibbutz* and its Arab neighbors was tense. In fact, he was named Moshe in memory of a neighbor, Moshe Barsky, a member of the commune who was killed by Arabs while riding home from a distant Jewish village, bringing medicine to his father. When Moshe was five, his parents left Degania and joined Nahalal, preferring a *moshav* to a *kibbutz*. (While in a *kibbutz* everything is communally owned and operated, and the children live in the communal children's home, the basic family unit is preserved in a *moshav*. Members have individual houses, where they live with their children, surrounded by their own livestock and their own small plots. The main production areas are operated by the co-operative which also markets all produce and operates the co-operative store.)

An old story has it that a young *kibbutz* member, when asked how he views the Arab problem, answers, "Through the sights of a rifle." This is how a youngster like Dayan, growing up in Nahalal, on the road from Haifa to Nazareth, must have seen the problem, too. Neighborly relations with the Arab villages in the vicinity were non-existent. Trouble over land and employment in the area was quite frequent; Arab shepherds tended to let their flocks graze on fields the settlers had brought forth with much sweat. Similar disputes had happened in Palestine since Cain slew Abel, causing bloodshed from the beginning of recorded history. But when the shepherds were Arabs, and the tillers of the soil were Jews, these occurrences became impregnated with national pride. The settlers were not only upset by the destruction the goats caused, but they also believed a passive attitude would make the Arabs lose respect for them, thus widening the breach between them. Therefore, the youngsters, armed with *naboots*, similar to the Arab shepherd's staff, used to fight it out. The technique of fighting with sticks, a kind of swordfighting called in Hebrew *kapap*, was a part of the essential equipment of every young Hebrew at the time.

When I lived in Nahalal in 1933 (when Dayan was eighteen), the village had a unique layout. The small, white square houses of the seventy-five member-families were situated in a perfect circle along a dirt road which disappeared during the winter in mud that reached halfway up to your knees. In the center were the co-operative institutions, including a civic hall where the theater would perform once a year. The transportation system consisted of one antiquated bus, which would go once a day through the hostile Arab villages to Haifa, operated by an old *moshav* member who sang arias and Russian songs all along the route. Both his sons were later killed during the 1948 war.

We school children would study a few hours a day, but most of the time we worked in the fields and vegetable gardens, helping the farmers who were all prematurely aged, their faces lined by years of ceaseless hard labor. In the evenings, around the petroleum table lamps, sometimes sipping homemade wine, they would recall the hard days when Nahalal was surrounded by malaria-infested swamps, which had to be reclaimed with eucalyptus trees.

At the age of fourteen Moshe was a watchman,

trained by the *Haganah*. (Actually, every member of a *kibbutz* and a *moshav* was automatically a member of the *Haganah*.) At eighteen he was sent to a neighboring village to instruct the youngsters there and lead them during an Arab attack. During the Arab rebellion of 1936, at age twenty-one, he commanded an instruction course of the Hebrew Auxiliary Police, a unit of *Haganah* members who were legalized by the British Administration for defense purposes. Two years before, he had married.

During the Arab rebellion Dayan met a man who had an everlasting influence on him, a British Army officer named Charles Orde Wingate.

Wingate, then only a captain, was one of those unorthodox characters produced by the British Army from time to time, a latter-day T. E. Lawrence. But while Lawrence had embraced the Arabs, Wingate embraced the Hebrews. A great leader of men, who always carried his Bible in his pocket, he invented the technique of retaliation raids, conducted by small units of selected, highly trained men, who would penetrate during the night deep into Arab territory, strike at a remote Arab village, demolish a few houses, sometimes kill some people, and return home before daylight. He was a single-minded, devoted man, quite ruthless, who sometimes scandalized the socialist *kibbutz* members by striking soldiers who had neglected some minute detail of preparation for action. Wingate's doctrine had a long-lasting effect on the *Haganah*. It formed the nucleus of the tactics of *Palmach*, the shock troop of the *Haganah* formed a few years later, and was transmitted by it to the Israeli Army. By then, Wingate was dead, accidentally killed during World War II after playing a brilliant role as guerrilla leader during the liberation of

Ethiopia and Burma and rising to the rank of major-general. It is likely that Dayan's character was formed in conscious imitation of this man—a war lover and individualist with a cult of toughness, a superman.

In 1939 Dayan was an instructor in a *Haganah* course. Along with the members of the course, he was captured by the British police during an illegal field exercise, carrying arms. In a mass trial, which became notorious as "The Trial of the 43," he was sentenced to five years in prison. While serving in Acre Prison, an old Crusader castle, he was suddenly called by the British to take part in the Syrian campaign; he went straight from prison into action. He lost his left eye on June 7, at the age of twenty-six, exactly twenty-six years before the soldiers under his direction reached the Suez Canal at the height of the Six-Day War.

* * *

Dayan's great hour might have come when the War of Liberation broke out at the end of 1947. During its first days his brother Zohar was killed while leading his men into action against a Druze ambush.

But oddly enough, during the 1948 war his star almost fell. His was not one of the great success stories of that war. The commanders of the new army, all of them *Haganah* veterans, never considered Moshe one of them, perhaps because he was a *Mapai* man in a closely knit group composed almost exclusively of left-wing officers. Also, he was not considered an outstanding tactician or responsible commander.

Thus, in the beginning of the war, no real command was given him. The high command, at long last, sent him on a rather undefined assignment to the Northern Front. There, as usual, he defied orders and acted on his own. Once he so outraged a local commander—one of the few foreign Jewish officers who had come as volunteers and held command posts in the new army—that Dayan was sentenced to be shot for insubordination. Only with great difficulty was this officer, a South African, convinced that this was not quite the way things were done in the *Haganah* army.

In the middle of the war, Dayan was sent abroad, on a purely decorative mission. The American Colonel David "Mickey" Marcus, also one of the foreign volunteers in the army, had been accidentally shot by a sentry at night. Dayan was sent to represent the Israeli government at the funeral in the United States, hardly an appropriate assignment for a dashing young commander at the height of a war.

He achieved his first great victory when he conquered the town of Lydda, nearly by accident. Taking the wrong turn, his motorized battalion dashed into the town, wildly shooting in all directions, and swamped the place before anyone realized what was happening. It was a great success, but it hardly established his reputation. His carefree, debonair way of making war never left Moshe. He was accused of mismanaging the battle of Kharatia in the Negev because his troop of jeeps and armored cars, an imitation of the by-now famous Samson's Foxes, never reached their objective, held up first by an armored car stuck in a narrow wadi. Waiting for it to be dragged out, Dayan lay down to sleep for a few minutes; when the time came, his soldiers couldn't find him among the bushes, losing valuable time. Subsequently, he was accused of failing to capture Bethlehem and Hebron when given the job to do so. In the latter part of the war he was appointed military commander of Jerusalem, a more diplomatic

than military job, because at the time fighting in that
sector had died down and negotiations with King Abdallah were in progress.

The end of the war might have brought an end to
Dayan's military career, as it did to the army career of
many of the more outstanding commanders. But Ben-
Gurion, who was re-organizing the army to eliminate
left-wing influences, decided otherwise. His disbanding
of the *Palmach* command, a carryover from the old
Haganah days, had just outraged the veterans and created a national controversy, never resolved. (Even
today, it is an Israeli joke to get up after a lecture,
during the question period, and ask the one question
guaranteed to bring the house down: "Why was the
Palmach disbanded?" It is a question which has no
parallel, except, perhaps, the Lavon Affair question:
"Who gave the order?") Ben-Gurion thought Dayan
would strengthen *Mapai* influence over the army and
also be loyal to him personally. He appointed him chief
of the southern command, and later, just before resigning for the first time, Chief of Staff. It was then that
Dayan became a public figure in his own right and the
symbol of the Israeli Army. As commander, he gave
the army an aggressive spirit, a doctrine of "when in
doubt, attack," a cavalry spirit in the tradition of
Rommel and Patton. On the other hand, he has not
been an organizing force, and his influence on team-
work was disruptive.

As a political leader Dayan was the apostle of "activism," believing as he does, that peace is an illusory
objective and that the Israeli-Arab conflict will last for
a long time. His attitude leads inevitably to the idea of
preventive war whenever the Arabs are in the process
of gaining the upper hand in the arms race or on the

verge of combining forces. While Dayan is not much more loyal to Ben-Gurion than he is to anyone else, he can be considered a direct successor, pupil and heir to Ben-Gurion, a Joshua to Ben-Gurion's Moses. Believing himself to be devoid of any ideology, he is nevertheless steeped in the philosophy of Ben-Gurion, so much so that he needn't be conscious of this orientation in order to act on it. Israelis associate Dayan with a Hebrew slang slogan which can be roughly translated into English as "bang and be done with it." This is the doctrine which led to the retaliation raids of 1953–56, and the Sinai Campaign, which turned Dayan into an international figure. The victory of 1956 established him as a great general. Actually, from a purely military point of view, it was a faulty campaign, not to be compared to the brilliant campaign of 1967, in which a vastly improved Israeli Army, without allies or foreign help, beat three Arab armies instead of one and reached the southern tip of Sinai in half the time.

* * *

Immediately after the 1956 war, Dayan finished his tour of duty as Chief of Staff and left the army. Some malicious tongues whispered that Ben-Gurion preferred to stand alone in the reviewing stand during the first Independence Day parade after the war.

What could a man like Dayan do outside the army? It was a bad time for him. At first he tried to study, listening to lectures at the Hebrew University of Jerusalem, sitting next to his daughter, another student, but he was not really interested. In 1959, he was included in the *Mapai* list for parliament, replacing his father, and was appointed Minister of Agriculture. In this post he managed to be as controversial as ever, without being considered very successful. The two ministries which he really wanted, Defense or Foreign, were held by members of the old guard, who in Israel, even more than anywhere else, are loath to turn over their posts to the younger people before being compelled to do so by the Divine Harvester.

The decline of Dayan was only a manifestation of the decline of activism as such. The retreat of the army from Sinai and Gaza following the astounding military victory of 1956 was a deep shock to the Israelis, intensified by the mere twenty-four hours between the victory announcement of Ben-Gurion, proclaiming the "Third Kingdom of Israel" and his speech announcing, in a broken voice, that he had acceded to President Eisenhower's request and agreed to the retreat. (The Third Kingdom referred to was meant to draw a line from the First Kingdom, that of David in biblical times; through the Second Kingdom, that of the Hasmonean Dynasty after the Maccabee Revolt against the successors of Alexander the Great, to a greater Israel of today. These terms correspond in time to the concept of First, Second and Third Temples.) The retreat seemed to show that military means had become obsolete as an instrument of policy in the Middle East. The fruits of victory—the opening of the Tiran Straits and the continued quiet on the southern frontier—seemed small indeed compared to the magnitude of the military success. Activism ceased to be fashionable in Israel for nearly ten years, until the sudden crisis immediately preceding the 1967 war.

In 1963 the cruelest blow befell Dayan. Without telling anyone beforehand, Ben-Gurion resigned. Dayan, whose political fortunes were bound up with those of Ben-Gurion, was left out in the cold. Ben-Gurion could easily have managed to establish him securely in the Ministry of Defense before resigning himself. But he did not care anymore. He was disillusioned with Dayan, as he was with everyone else, because Dayan failed to support him vigorously in his request to re-open the Lavon Affair. Thus, Dayan, still the thankless Minister of Agriculture, was left without any political support. After a time, he resigned, an unusual thing in Israel, hinting vaguely at disagreements with Eshkol.

While Ben-Gurion set about disrupting the *Mapai* party and setting up his own party, which Dayan joined only at the last possible moment and then under duress, Dayan became more and more impatient. As his daughter tells it, "When political life relegated him to the back benches of the opposition, he became irritable and restless. He was born for action, for being in the center of events, for showing people the way."

The new *Rafi* party, representing eight per cent of the vote, was hardly the center of events, nor was it showing the people any well defined way. Prospects seemed bleak indeed. Out of sheer boredom, one suspects, and in order again to attract some attention, Dayan went to Viet Nam as a widely publicized war correspondent. His daughter goes on: "He found some release in his trip to Viet Nam. When he came back, the question arose again, 'What to do now?'."

The answer was provided by Gamal Abd-el-Nasser. Immediately before the crisis, in a public opinion poll in which people were asked who they would prefer as Prime Minister, Dayan got only fourteen per cent (a not very impressive result, considering that even I got seven per cent). Now, suddenly faced with what looked like mortal danger, a strong, young, energetic, charismatic war leader was needed—not to conduct the war,

but to fulfill a psychological need. Under great public
pressure, Dayan was appointed Minister of Defense two
days after his fifty-second birthday. When the news was
announced over the radio, soldiers jumped out of their
trenches to embrace each other, and an audible sigh of
relief filled the air. The man who had been fighting
Arabs all his life was predestined for this hour.

* * *

What part did Dayan really play in the war? Many
things have been written about this, most of them unin-
formed.

To many, especially to quickie war correspondents,
Dayan is the man who single-handedly decided on the
war and waged it, a kind of latter-day Julius Caesar
who came, saw and conquered, the military genius, the
desert fox. To others, he looked like a kind of stunt
man, a Johnny-come-lately whose real genius lay in the
field of public relations. Levi Eshkol has intimated that
Dayan, while having had a salutary effect on morale,
had nothing to do with the war itself.

The truth lies somewhere in between. It is true that
Dayan had irritated many people by his penchant for
publicity, claiming undue credit for himself, or, at least,
not disclaiming the credit given him by foreign correspondents who thought that the one-eyed general would
make so much better copy than some anonymous professional strategist. During the war itself, Dayan seems
to have had enough time on his hands to rush around
like an errant comet, dragging behind him a long tail of
public relations officers, correspondents and photogra-
phers, who immortalized him, with the backdrop provided by the advancing combat units.

Yet it would be unjust to disclaim the very real part which Dayan played in this dramatic event.

He had nothing to do with preparing the army for the war. For ten years he had been outside the army. A new team, composed of the junior officers of the 1948 war, had produced an efficient, professional, well-trained army, equipped with the instruments needed for the tactics they had decided to employ in case of war. The Israeli Army believes in improvisation, a system well-suited to the Israeli character. It, therefore, has no great master plan, but rather a large number of limited contingency plans, which can be arbitrarily combined in case of need. The actual team which conducted the war, presided over by General Rabin, was an outstanding group of professionals, most of them quite unassuming, not one of them indispensable.

At the beginning of the crisis, when war already seemed probable, Dayan asked to be allowed to visit the command posts on the southern front and study their plans. His request was granted by Eshkol. Thus Dayan was already well acquainted with all command decisions of the planning stage. Upon assuming the post of Minister of Defense, he was able to review these plans immediately.

He made two significant changes on the southern front. The first concerned strategy. Originally it was envisioned to send two divisions into combat against the Egyptians, keeping the third in reserve. Dayan—convinced by his own experience of 1956 that after the breakthrough, the Egyptians would be unable, practically and psychologically, to mount a counter-attack—decided to send in the third division with the first wave. This shortened the campaign and, perhaps, enabled the army to reach the Canal before the U.N. could react. The second decision was tactical. It had been proposed to land paratroopers by helicopters near Um Katef, a decisive location. This plan had been overruled by the General Staff as potentially too costly in lives. Dayan reinstated the original plan and was proved right.

On the other hand, Dayan was an inhibiting force on the other two fronts. When the Old City of Jerusalem was encircled, he was against a frontal attack on it. On the insistence of other Cabinet members, but against Dayan's wishes, this attack was mounted, thereby gaining all of Jerusalem before the cease-fire came into effect. On the Syrian front, Dayan delayed the attack for forty-eight hours, against the express wish of the Cabinet and the local commanders. Dayan wanted to concentrate a much larger force for this operation, the most difficult one of the war. This enabled new troops to rush from the Jordanian to the Syrian front. No one who saw it will ever forget the mad scramble of units, in commandeered taxis and trucks, in seemingly utter disorder, in a race against time, yet sorting itself out effortlessly at the moment of attack. It was the Israeli Army at its unique best. However, if the Baathist government sits today in Damascus, it can thank Dayan. Without his intervention, Damascus would certainly have been captured before the cease-fire became effective.

On the grand decision to start the war, Dayan had little influence, and no influence was needed. His being co-opted in the government was already a part of the resolve to put an end to the crisis by attacking the Egyptians, a decision with which the whole country agreed, and which, by that time, had become inevitable.

But his presence certainly stiffened this resolve, dispelling the last doubts.

* * *

Where is Dayan going now? The Ministry of Defense is a focal point in Israeli politics, embodying as it does, a great concentration of power. But its Minister is not necessarily the crown prince of Israeli politics. Whether Dayan will attain his obvious objective, the Prime Ministry, depends very much upon the turn of events and the changing mood of the country. A public opinion poll immediately after the war, showed, significantly, that while more than eighty per cent of the people approved of Dayan's conduct as Minister of Defense, only twenty per cent preferred him as Prime Minister, with an equal percentage of the public voting for Abba Eban.

If Israel emerges from the present phase as a chauvinistic, extremist country, convinced that future wars with the Arabs are inevitable, Dayan might well become Prime Minister by 1969. If, on the contrary, a more moderate mood prevails, Dayan might find himself the leader of an activist minority, bypassed by history.

Dayan has been vocal but self-contradictory on the central question of what to do with the occupied territories. During the first two months after the war, he made half a dozen statements on this subject, each canceling the other. He has advocated, alternately, the setting up of an autonomous Palestinian state, a federation between Israel and Jordan, and the annexation of Gaza and the West Bank of the Jordan.

In his great speech at the opening of the last *Rafi*

conference in December 1967, he proposed a six-point program of singular ambiguity. The points were:

1) "to safeguard the Jewish character of the State of Israel, in its composition and population";

2) "to secure the recognition of Israel as a sovereign Jewish state by its neighbors";

3) "to achieve international equality of rights in the region, including freedom of navigation in all international waterways";

4) "to design new frontiers, which will safeguard the territorial integrity and the sovereignty of the state";

5) "to create frontiers which will express the bond of the Jewish people to its historical homeland";

6) "to strive for peace-agreements with the Arab states, in the context of which the Arab refugee question will also be settled."

If this sounds rather obscure to the reader of English, so it sounded to the Hebrew listener. The points could well mean outright annexation of all conquered territories. The phrase "historical homeland" is associated in Hebrew with the concept of the "historical Eretz-Israel," which includes both banks of the Jordan. The emphasis on the Jewish character of the state could mean denying citizenship to the Arabs. On the other hand, the same points, read differently, could mean the setting up of a Palestinian state, federated with Israel, or at least an autonomous "Palestinian Arab entity," which would safeguard the Jewish character and the security of Israel, and leave a bond between Israel and the rest of Palestine. It could also mean giving the West Bank back to King Hussein, with boundary changes and some special status for the West Bank.

Which interpretation is right? Nobody, perhaps not even Dayan himself, knows for sure. While many believe that Dayan would really like to create a kind of Arab canton under Israeli suzerainty in the West Bank, thus keeping Israel itself Jewish but opening new territory for Jewish colonization, there were passages in the Dayan speech which went back to the way of thinking of the old Arab-fighter.

A few days before, the writer Yishar Smilansky, a prominent member of the *Rafi* party, had sharply attacked the poets who are clamoring for annexation and "the whole Eretz-Israel." Dayan, in this speech, vigorously disagreed with Smilansky, justifying the arguments of the Greater Israel proponents. In a revealing passage he said: "I myself have been brought up on the slogan 'dunam after dunam, goat after goat,' and not on the slogan 'In blood and fire did Judea fall, in blood and fire will Judea rise again.' But the fact is that since 1936 all that we achieved was secured through the force of arms."

"Dunam after dunam," as we have seen, was the motto of the socialist Zionist colonizing movement, the "practical" Zionism to which Dayan's family belonged, while the song of "blood and fire" was sung by the *Irgun* and the Revisionists, who opposed this brand of Zionism. (1936 was the year the Arab rebellion broke out.) By justifying, in retrospect, the slogan of the opposing camp, Dayan proclaimed a credo which can lead to the conclusion: If everything was achieved until now by war—why should we be interested in peace now? Why shouldn't we expect further gains in future wars?

Dayan did not say so, but, in the same speech, he rejected any hope for peace with the Arabs in the foreseeable future. In a manner reminiscent of the Roy Rotenberg funeral speech, he declared that the Six-Day War made peace even more remote, that the Arabs could not be expected to recognize an Israel which had become even stronger and bigger, and which now holds territory forty miles from Damascus. Dayan, of course, excluded any possibility of retreat from these territories.

From time to time Dayan plays these days with the idea of becoming a Man of Peace, of competing for leadership as a hawk-turned-dove. He likes to show himself as the man to whom the Arabs in the occupied territories can talk. As the minister in charge of the military administration in these territories, which, on the whole, conducts itself in an admirably liberal way, he can pose as a liberal himself.

But, I believe, that after every such intermezzo, Dayan will always return to his original image—the Arab-fighter. And he himself certainly senses that he can achieve supreme power in the next few years only if a new war-like situation creates a renewed popular demand for a strong man at the helm.

* * *

The man Moshe Dayan is a typical Israeli, a product of Hebrew nationalism. He personifies certain facets of the Israeli character, traits which are latent, in one combination or another, in the mental makeup of every Israeli who has grown up in the country. But like a character in a well-written play, he is a man in whom the traits of ordinary people have become crystallized, magnified, and perhaps exaggerated.

Israel might become Dayanized, or it might become something quite different. Whether it will go one way or the other, now that it stands at the crossroads, depends upon how it solves the inner conflicts to which the next part of this book is devoted.

PART TWO

The Breaking Out

9: The Mistake of Columbus

On October 12, 1492, Columbus landed on a Bahama island called Guanahani by the Indians—and discovered the New World.

But Columbus did not have the slightest idea what he'd done. Nothing was farther from his mind than discovering new worlds; it was the oldest of worlds he was looking for—India and the spice islands. A new world was not an economic proposition, and one may wonder whether the whole expedition would have come about if the result had been foreseen.

Yet, using only the crudest of instruments, knowing very little about geography, his head crammed with false ideas, Columbus bravely sailed forth into the unknown and inadvertently changed the shape of the world.

Something like this happened to Zionism, and therein lie the causes of all its inner conflicts, as well as the solutions to its problems.

Zionism set out with the idea that the Jews of the world constitute a nation—a nation in the European sense, a group of people who identify themselves with a political state, either an existing one or one to be established. Starting from this assumption, the problem was one of transportation, in the widest sense: once a Jewish homeland in Palestine was created, all Jews, or at least most of them, would go there to live in Herzl's *Judenstaat*.

History has proved this theory false. A Jewish state was indeed set up in Palestine, but the great majority of Jews has not shown any undue inclination to go there. Two and a half million, most acting under diverse forms of duress, have indeed settled in what is now Israel. But several million others, who were not subject to physical persecution, stayed where they were. Immigration is near a standstill, with only the wish of Soviet Jewry, not allowed to leave its closed society, still in doubt.

It seems, therefore, that world Jewry is not a nation, in the Zionist sense. This would have spelled the failure of the Zionist experiment, if something quite unforeseen had not happened in the meantime: A new nation was, indeed, born in Palestine.

Looking back today, this seems to have been as inevitable as the discovery of the New World, once Columbus and his little fleet left the shores of Europe on a westward course. If you transfer hundreds of thousands of people to a foreign land—a new climate and landscape—in which they speak a newly resurrected language and respond to different physical and political challenges, the stage is set for the emergence of a new society. If this society has a sense of political destiny and unity, it becomes a new nation. This has happened in the United States, in Australia, in Brazil, in many other countries. It has happened in Palestine.

We, the sons and daughters of Zionism, are indeed a new nation, not just another part of world Jewry that happens to live in Palestine. This is the central fact of our life, obscured by obsolete ideas and slogans, a truth that must be grasped if anything about our existence, our problems, and our future is to be understood.

What is a nation? Many answers have been given to this question, each influenced by the particular ideology of its proponent. Some put the emphasis on a common territory, others on a common culture or economy. I don't believe in abstract formulas to which life has to be somehow adapted. To me the answer seems simple and pragmatic: A nation is a group of people who believe that they are a nation, who want to live as a nation, have a common political destiny, identify themselves with a political state, pay its taxes, serve in its army, work for its future, share its fate—and, if necessary, die for it.

In this sense, we in Israel are a nation, unmistakably and irrevocably, for better or for worse. Our nation comprises all of us, from Dan to Elat, but it does not include a Jew in Brooklyn, Paris or Bucharest, much as he may sympathize with our country and feel an affinity for it.

The difference between Jewish fathers anywhere in the world and Israeli sons is much more than the usual contradiction between generations; it is a mutation. A different mode of life, nutrition, climate, political reality and social environment could not but make the Palestinian-born son vastly unlike his ghetto-born father. It is not uncommon for a young Israeli in the United States or Europe to hear the exclamation: "But you don't look like a Jew!" This dubious "compliment" still carries a grain of truth. The robust, tall, often dark-

blond and blue-eyed *sabra*, is, indeed, even externally
different from his Jewish ancestors, much as the average Australian or American differs from his English
great-grandfather. Jewish culture, created in the Diaspora by a persecuted, religious-minded minority, does
not appeal to an Israeli generation which has a somewhat exaggerated sense of freedom. That part of the
Jewish religion based on the Talmud and the Halacha,
both products of the Diaspora, has in Israel degenerated into party slogans; the Bible, however, the most
powerful book in Hebrew literature, is immensely popular, and archeology became a national fad long before
Moshe Dayan started to dig. Significantly, in day-to-day
modern Hebrew usage, Israelis have unconsciously
come to use the term *Jewish* when they mean foreign
Jews or new immigrants or religion, and to call *Hebrew*
everything connected with themselves: We never speak
about the Jewish army, the Jewish nation, the Jewish
settlement or Jewish labor, but the Hebrew army, the
Hebrew nation, the Hebrew settlement and Hebrew
labor. Thus, long before the *idea* of a new *Hebrew*
nation had evolved, it had become an unconsciously
accepted fact.

We are a new nation, the Hebrew nation, whose
homeland is Palestine (which we call Eretz-Israel) and
whose political creation is the State of Israel.

This does not mean, except for a small lunatic fringe,
that we want to turn our backs on world Jewry and cut
ourselves off from it. As the period of the Six-Day War
has clearly demonstrated, there is a very real and profound feeling of solidarity between Jews all over the
world and Israel. We are grateful for this and recipro-
cate it. Solidarity there is. Affinity there is. But world
Jewry is not a nation, while the Hebrew Israelis are.

It is never quite accurate to draw an analogy between different peoples, because there are no two quite alike. Yet, to illustrate a point, one could say that the relationship between Israelis and Jews is like that between Australians and Englishmen. Australia has a deep sense of affinity for Great Britain; in two world wars, Australia rushed to the defense of England long before it was threatened itself. Some Australians, even today, say "home" when they mean England. Yet there can be no doubt that Australia is a nation by itself, with its own special interests, trying to respond to its own particular challenges, conducting a national policy suited to its own geo-political circumstances (as its participation in the war in Viet Nam has shown).

Thus, Zionism created something which it never consciously intended, a new nation. And by its very success, Zionism has become obsolete; by attaining its goals, Zionism provided for its own negation.

* * *

The existence of a new nation, Middle Eastern by birth, makes an entirely different approach to the Israeli-Arab problem possible. Unfortunately, this has yet to become clear to both Arab and Israeli. It is a common historical phenomenon that the ideological superstructure of a society, what the French call *mystique*, may linger on long after the reality upon which it was based has disappeared and made a new approach necessary.

An ideology is not just a set of ideas which can be changed easily. It is bound up with vested interests on many different levels. It exists in the textbooks of schools and in the mental set of generations of teachers, thereby molding the minds of boys and girls born into a

new reality. Social institutions, with their hosts of functionaries and economic enterprises, are based upon ideology. Political parties fighting for the advantages of
political power perpetuate the philosophies imprinted
on them since their inception; this is particularly true in
Israel, all of whose political parties were founded in
Europe before their leaders even came to the country.
It is natural that a political regime which led Zionism to
its heroic period is not one to relinquish power volun-
tarily and easily. The Zionist ideological and political
superstructure, therefore, still exerts an immense influence in Israel. The establishment of the state has not
changed this; indeed, it has changed very little in the
personal and political composition of the leading class
in the country. Therefore it is very difficult to answer a
question like: "Is Israel a Zionist state?"

For many young people in Israel, the word *Zionism*
is derogatory. In *sabra* slang, "to talk Zionism" means
to talk nonsense, to use highfaluting slogans devoid of
concrete meaning. To the practical *sabra* mind, pragmatic by nature, it has long been obvious that some
fundamental tenets of Zionism have not stood the test
of time; yet these same *sabras* may unconsciously cling
to Zionist ideas which they know to have been proved
false.

The fundamental tenets of Zionism can be defined as
follows: (a) all the Jews in the world are one nation;
(b) Israel is a Jewish state, created by the Jews and for
the Jews all over the world; (c) the Jewish dispersal is
a temporary situation, and sooner or later all Jews will
have to come to Israel, driven, if by nothing else, by
inevitable anti-Semitic persecution; (d) the Ingathering
of these Exiles is the *raison d'être* of Israel, the primary
purpose to which all other aims have to be subservient.

This line is taught in Israeli schools, propounded in political speeches, written in the press. It is the essence of the existing regime.

Yet nothing could be further from what young Israelis believe in. Theirs is a different outlook, an Israeli nationalism pure and simple, sometimes moderate and sometimes extreme, but a nationalism very similar to any other one, bound up with the fortunes of the State of Israel, its territory, its language, its culture and its army.

The two different sets of ideals can co-exist only because the gap between them seldom becomes obvious. Yet it is real and has a profound, if hidden, influence on the day-to-day conduct of affairs.

* * *

Let's take, for example, the question of religion.

Few people are as non-religious, even anti-religious, as the great majority of Israelis, but in few countries has organized religion such a stranglehold on life. While Jews in America are the most extreme defenders of the principle of the separation of church and state, this idea is considered heresy in Israel, for a very elementary reason: The Declaration of Independence, promulgated on May 14, 1948, proclaims Israel to be a Jewish state, and this is embedded in the legal structure of Israel. The Law of Return gives every Jew the automatic right to come and settle in Israel. A second law confers Israeli citizenship upon every Jewish immigrant the minute he enters the country, unless he undergoes a specific procedure waiving his right; if he happens to be married to a Christian, this right is not conferred on his spouse, who must acquire citizenship by the normal process of naturalization.

Yet what is a Jew? Who is a Jew? No clear-cut legal definition exists. Nor can there exist any definition but a religious one. Throughout the ages, Jews were a religious community. In fact, the courts of Israel have decided that a person ceases to be a Jew if he adopts another religion—a decision which makes it clear that being Jewish is basically a religious thing. If so, the argument runs, how can there be a separation between synagogue and state? If Israel exists for world Jewry, if its main aim is to ingather these Jews who are organized as a religious community, how can the concept of a Jewish nation be separated from the Jewish religion? Indeed, those of us in Israel who fight for the separation of synagogue and state are constantly accused of trying to sever Israel from world Jewry, turning it into just another small Levantine state. Thus, not one of the big, old Zionist parties advocates such a separation. All of them declare state and religion, nation and religion, to be one in the unique case of the Jews.

The minority in Israel who are religious, therefore, have a power quite disproportionate to their numerical strength. Only about fifteen per cent of the population voted for the three religious parties represented in the *Knesset,* giving them seventeen out of 120 seats in the 1965 elections. But by Israeli law there is neither civil marriage nor civil divorce, these affairs being within the sole dominion of the Rabbinate (and the functionaries of other religious groups, as far as their people are concerned). A Jew cannot marry a Christian or a Moslem, nor can a Jew named Cohen marry a divorced woman. Cohens or those with similar names are assumed to belong to the ancient families of priests, who are forbidden by Jewish law to marry anyone but a virgin: in theory, they might be called upon someday to officiate again in a new Temple. One cannot abdicate this right even if one wishes to—once a Cohen, always a Cohen. (In fact, a justice of the Israeli Supreme Court, a sophisticated man named Chaim Cohen, had to go to the United States in order to marry a divorced woman; and the validity of this marriage is extremely doubtful under the laws which he himself has to administer!) Neither busses nor the railway operate in Israel from sundown Friday until the first three stars appear in the sky on Saturday evening (but everyone can travel, in private cars and via a highly organized taxi service, along the exact routes of the busses). The law forbids the raising of pigs in all parts of the country except those where Christian Arabs constitute a local majority (yet one can easily buy pork anywhere in Israel, and pork steaks—euphemistically called "White steaks" or "French steaks"—can be clandestinely obtained at Tel Aviv steak-stands).

It is a situation of many paradoxes, with controversy and clashes, extremely irritating to the vast majority of the people. Yet these same people accept the situation as natural and inevitable, forced to this conclusion by the concept of oneness of religion and nation. Only the repudiation of this concept by Israeli nationalism, an ever-growing factor in Israeli life, will eventually lead to Israel's becoming a normal secular state.

* * *

Religion also plays a great role—even if a largely unconscious one—in the demographic dynamism of Israel. Any foreigner coming to Israel is immediately struck by the incredible variety of racial types in the streets. There are Jews of many colors, all the way from Nordic white to Ethiopian black, with many shades of brown in between. Ours is obviously a very non-racial kind of society.

Anyone considered a Jew is easily absorbed in Israel. While it is quite true that much hidden, often unconscious, discrimination exists between the communities, one should not exaggerate its importance. Jews of European descent, generally called *Ashkenazim* (from the Hebrew name for medieval middle and northern Europe) may look with condescension upon Jews of Mediterranean and Eastern descent, generally called *Sephardim* (from *Sepharad*, the Hebrew name for Spain). These are considered culturally inferior and educationally backward, and Ashkenazi parents will often object to their offspring marrying Sephardim. Yet discrimination like this exists in many countries: a comparison which comes to mind is the attitude of Northern Italians toward their Sicilian compatriots. The essential facts are that no Israeli, with the possible exception of a handful of crackpots, will consciously justify such discrimination and that it disappears in times of national stress, such as the recent war. For Zionists, a Jew is a Jew, wherever he comes from and whatever his mother tongue, the concept of Jewishness overriding other considerations. (In this respect, at least, there is little difference between Zionism and Israeli nationalism. An Israeli nationalist deplores the division among communities even more than Zionists do, believing that the common language, common culture, and community of political destiny of the new nation should abolish differences brought by the immigrants from their countries of origin.) It seems virtually certain that this kind of discrimination will disappear in time and constitute no real danger to the state, irksome as it may be right now.

A different situation prevails, however, as far as non-Jews are concerned. The idea of a homogeneous Jewish state is inherent in Zionism. A state which exists for the solution of the Jewish problem should be populated, so the Zionists feel, by Jews. Any non-Jew is really a foreign element in the present Israeli regime. Non-Jewish immigrants, even non-Jewish spouses of Jewish immigrants, find great obstacles to their absorption into Israeli society. Here, Zionist religionism and Israeli nationalism part. In modern times it should be easy to join a nation, the average Israeli feels: if you want to be a part of Hebrew society, speak its language, bring up your children in its culture, support its state, and serve in its army, you should be welcome. For a Zionist, this idea is unacceptable. You can become a Jew only by undergoing a religious ritual—circumcision for men, immersion in water in a religious bathhouse for women, with all the accompanying religious ritual.

While this question may only be important to the few non-Jewish immigrants, the idea of a homogeneous Jewish state has grave consequences for Arabs. It was not only a question of security and political allegiance which made it impossible for Israel to integrate the 300,000 Arabs living in it before the 1967 war. Far more operative, though seldom mentioned, was the instinctive conviction of old-time Zionists that Arabs could never really be a part of a state which was Jewish. For anyone entertaining this conviction, the idea of repatriating Arab refugees and increasing the Arab minority was positively obnoxious.

Prior to the 1967 war, Ben-Gurion's closest adherents started an outcry against the possibility that the Arab minority—then less than twelve per cent—would eventually become a majority in Israel by natural increase, a process which would have taken them several generations, even on the unlikely assumption that their present high birthrate would continue interminably. But it is not only the fear of an Arab majority which set Zionists against any idea of refugee repatriation, but the deeply felt, if quite often unconscious, conviction that Jews should be alone in their state, that Israel should remain homogeneously Jewish, that the Arab minority, if inevitable, should at least be kept as small as possible.

Before June 1967, the Arab minority, while constituting nearly twelve per cent of the population, held only two per cent of the posts in the government administration, with not one single Arab among the top-ranking officials, judges or cabinet ministers. Among the 120 members of the *Knesset*, only seven are Arabs, not one of whom occupies an important position in the House. (My first move after election, on the very first day of the 1967 *Knesset*, was to propose that the Speaker, or at least one of his eight deputies, should be an Arab. This was indignantly rejected.)

It is, in truth, while exploring the wider problem of Israeli-Arab relations that the gap between the Zionist philosophy and a normal healthy Hebrew nationalism becomes apparent.

* * *

Nothing frightens the Arabs more than the idea of the Ingathering of the Exiles. There arises before Arab eyes the spectre of a wave of Jewish immigration, bringing to Israel another ten million Jews, overflowing its narrow frontiers and conquering Arab states, evicting the inhabitants and grabbing land for innumerable new *kibbutzim*. There is something ludicrous in the present situation. Zionists leaders, including Prime Minister Eshkol, make visionary speeches about millions of Jews who will soon arrive on the shores of Israel, fulfilling the prophesy of Zionism. To an Israeli audience, knowing the reality, this is the sort of wishful thinking by which an antiquated regime tries desperately to preserve its obsolete slogans. Yet, to millions of Arabs these speeches sound like definite threats to Arab existence, threats made even more terrible by Israel's manifest military superiority.

Thus an empty slogan can become a political factor in the most negative sense.

But the Zionist philosophy has a more destructive influence on Israel's own mentality. Because a Zionist considers Israel the beachhead of world Jewry, world Jewry is seen as an inexhaustible reservoir of manpower and money; thus, the relationship between Israel and the Jews, mainly in the West, seems of primary importance, while that between Israel and the Arab world automatically, therefore, takes a back seat. The location of Israel in the Middle East seems a geographical accident, to be disregarded whenever possible, dealt with by military means if necessary. The ideal solution for a Zionist would be to saw off Israel from the Middle East and tow it away to a more congenial environment, somewhere opposite the French Riviera —if not off Long Island or near Miami Beach.

How else can one explain the most astonishing fact in Israeli public life? After a Zionist-Arab conflict which has gone on for three generations, and the actual state of war between Israel and the Arab states which is now entering its twentieth year, there does not exist an effective government department for Arab affairs. While we have a Ministry for Posts and a Ministry for

Transportation, to say nothing of a Ministry for Tourism and a Ministry for Police, we don't have a Ministry for Middle Eastern Affairs. These are relegated to the Foreign Ministry, whose primary job is to defend Israel in the international arena from the political onslaught of the Arabs and, therefore, has nothing much to do with making contact with the Arab world and creating an atmosphere of peace. Indeed, such a task requires quite different approaches and talents. All the dealings between Israel and the Arab countries, all political initiatives from Israel toward the Arab world, are the proper province of the department for Middle Eastern affairs in the Foreign Ministry. But this department employs only thirty out of 900 officials in the Foreign Office, out of a total number of government employees well over 50,000, excluding policemen and teachers. Even this figure of thirty is misleading. If we deduct from it the personnel dealing with non-Arab Middle Eastern countries, such as Iran, and the purely clerical jobs, there are but three or four officials left to deal with what obviously is the main problem of Israel.

The 1967–68 budget of the government of Israel exceeds five billion Israeli pounds. Of this sum, less than 0.05 per cent—or less than three per cent of the expenditure of the Foreign Office—is devoted to Middle Eastern affairs. This sum again includes the Israeli activities in Iran, which are extensive, as well as clerical expenses.

Such a neglect of Israeli-Arab affairs would be impossible, after all that has happened, were it not for the Zionist image of an Israel oriented toward Western Jewry and the West in general. Of all the legacies Zionism bequeathed to the State of Israel, this is perhaps the most dangerous.

The new Hebrew generation has necessarily a different view of its place in the world. It has grown up in Palestine. It knows that it belongs to a new nation born in Palestine. It does not look at the Middle East from the outside, but from the inside. In fact, it has abolished the term Middle East in Hebrew usage: Middle East is a European term, assuming the center of the world to be somewhere in the West, but it is ridiculous for an Israeli to talk about the Middle East when he means, for example, countries like Algeria or even Egypt, which lie to our west. Therefore, when we started to talk about a Hebrew nation instead of a Jewish nation, we also started to talk about the Semitic region, or simply The Region (*ha-merkhav*) instead of the Middle East.

Belonging to The Region means dealing with the central problem of our existence—the Arabs—either by military or by political means, either through war or through peace. We Israelis, who have been born into this problem, know that we must solve it—we all know it, from Moshe Dayan, identified with the warlike approach, to people like me, standing for the opposite. We don't wrack our brains trying to find a solution to the Jewish Question, real or imaginary; the central task of our generation is to integrate our nation into the framework of our region.

We are nationalists. To Western ears this word has a negative coloring. Indeed, to anyone from the older Western nations, nationalism is an unconscious part of a mental set; such a person can even consciously believe that nationalism belongs to the past and is an evil to be overcome.

Yet nationalism simply means that in the world of today, individuals, except for perhaps a handful of uni-

versal geniuses, function within national political
frameworks and national cultures. In the best sense,
nationalism, defending its own national rights, recognizes the national rights of others. It is only in its exag-
gerations, in its imperialist or fascist forms which try
to suppress other nations, that nationalism becomes a
destructive force.

Even extreme nationalists, such as Dayan, recognize
the national aspirations of the Arabs, something our
Zionist fathers were unable or unwilling to take into
account.

The emergence, then, of a young nationalist generation, superseding Zionism, creates the psychological
basis for a solution.

10: *The Establishment*

POLITICAL SOLUTIONS have to be put into operation by political forces. Therefore, before examining the solutions proposed, let us analyze first the composition of political life in Israel and the currents at work. Much has been written about this, but little is known, for Israeli political forces are quite different from what they seem to be to the superficial foreign observer— even more so than other aspects of Israeli life.

We have an apparently bewildering array of parties in Israel. During the 1965 elections, eleven election lists got enough votes to be represented in the present *Knesset*. Two of these lists comprised two parties each, aligning themselves for tactical purposes. The biggest list won forty-five of the *Knesset's* 120 seats, the smallest won only one seat.

This variety of political forces is the result of proportional representation: the whole state is considered one big constituency, and the seats are divided among all the election lists according to the number of votes each receives. Thus, no votes are lost, unlike the American and British systems, in which the winner takes all and the votes backing losers are wasted. Proportional representation allows every minority to have a voice, and it is very difficult, therefore, for any single party to receive an absolute majority. Even at the height of Ben-Gurion's power, his *Mapai* never received more than forty per cent of the vote. The biggest party is called upon to make a coalition agreement with other parties who control at least enough additional votes to create a majority for the government. Negotiations for a government coalition are always prolonged and difficult. Smaller parties will bargain their support for pieces of legislation in which they are particularly interested. (Because of this, religious parties, for example, can generally trade in their votes for another piece of religious coercion, obnoxious to the majority.)

In reality, all this works out not very differently from the American system. In the United States, however, the deals are usually made within one big party, or between the two. In Israel, they are made among several party secretariats. But party members in the *Knesset* are rigidly controlled by their leaders and it is a rare sight indeed to see a *Knesset* member vote against his party. Once the parties of the government coalition agree on a piece of legislation, the actual passage in parliament becomes a mere formality.

Even the political variety is more superficial than it seems. Of the eleven parliamentary groups elected in 1965, all but five deputies (four Communists and I) are Zionists. They are united on every important issue, divided only on questions of implementation. The differences between Menachem Begin, the right-wing Zionist *Herut* party leader and Meir Yaari, the left-wing Zionist *Mapam* leader are certainly smaller than those between a racist Democratic Senator from Alabama and a liberal Democratic senator from New York. Actually, all the Zionist parties could well fit into the U.S. Democratic Party, with some room to spare on both sides.

The party set-up changes frequently; parties split, unite, change names, set up blocks and alignments in the most bewildering manner. On the eve of the last elections, three parties split, four parties set up two "alignments" with different names. Since then, three parties have united into one, with a new name, the Israel Labor Party, and everyone else seems to be casting his eyes around for new blocs, even while new splits threaten his own party.

The maneuvering obscures the central fact of political life in Israel—a well-nigh incredible stability. In spite of all the new names, splits and alignments, nothing at all has changed fundamentally in the political life of the Hebrew community in Palestine since the early Thirties. All the new parties are but splinters or continuations of old ones, and every Zionist political group can trace its origin back to the beginning of the century.

* * *

A few years ago, Kadish Luz, the widely respected Speaker of the *Knesset*, made a speech which received much publicity. Reviewing the political scene, he expressed astonishment at the fact that no change at all in the division of power had been effected since the establishment of the state, despite the fact that since then, the population had increased three-fold, with two new immigrants for each citizen who was there in 1948. The new immigrants seem to have easily fallen into the party pattern which was already there, leaving each party with exactly the same percentage of the votes as it had before.

The explanation for this phenomenon lies in the particular character of the Israeli parties, which do not resemble parties in any other country. Ideally, a party is a voluntary association of citizens who unite in order to further a particular outlook or interest. Ideally again, the members support the party with their contributions, elect its leadership and control it. Nothing of this applies to the Zionist parties, which have power structures almost independent of their members, controlled by professional leaders and financed by outside sources.

To paraphrase Mirabeau's famous dictum about the army in Prussia: Elsewhere, the state has parties; in Israel, the parties have a state. The machinery of the great parties is by far more powerful and entrenched than the machinery of the state, and for a reason: the parties existed long before the State of Israel was created. The state is a newcomer on the scene, the parties are not. If we trace the origin of the parties, we find that the youngest was born in the early Twenties. The Revisionist Party, set up by Jabotinsky in opposition to Weizmann, changed its name in 1948 to the *Herut* Movement (*herut* meaning liberty) and in 1965 created a bloc with the Liberal Party, now called, for short, *Gahal*. After forty-five years, this party has not changed an iota of its official ideology—and during this time, it has not changed its proportion of the voters, about fifteen per cent.

A Zionist party, forty years ago, was unlike any other party in the world. It had to be. Its main job was not to gather votes in an existing constituency; it was to create a constituency. The typical party would be centered somewhere in Poland, recruiting members there and trying to convince as many of them as possible to go to Palestine. To help them emigrate, it collected money all over Europe and the United States and set up economic apparatus. To help its members settle in Israel, it set up there another apparatus, dealing with housing, health insurance, education, and the provision of jobs. This typical party, forty years ago, had certain characteristics which were the outcome of these circumstances. Most of its leaders lived abroad. Its ideology originated there, without much connection with the realities of Palestine, certainly without any bearing on the Arab problem. It was controlled by a closely knit group of founders, who, in turn, controlled a growing financial apparatus based abroad and operating in Palestine. It would, in short, control its members rather than receive direction from them.

As yet, there was no state. The Zionist leadership had no police force, no prisons, none of the ordinary means to implement its laws and directives—but it had the parties and *their* institutions. Thus, the parties became, quite consciously, instruments of control equipped with some of the powers and functions ordinarily reserved for states.

Members who wanted to break party discipline could not simply vote for someone else. They might be members of the *kibbutz* belonging to a party, and leaving the *kibbutz* meant abandoning a home, a job, security, a circle of friends, practically everything that makes up the life of a family, to start a completely new life in the unknown world outside. (The *kibbutz* would generally be composed of a group of people who had known each other since childhood, might have come to Palestine as a group, and belonged to the same party. Until quite recently, it was impossible for a *kibbutz* member to belong to a different party from his fellow *kibbutzniks*, as the commune itself was an integral part of the party machinery. Even today, in some of the *Mapam kibbutzim*, a witch hunt starts after every election to find out who the three or four anonymous dissidents were.) Outside the *kibbutz*, conditions were less extreme but not different. A party member would live in a party housing scheme, work at a job provided by the party labor exchange and controlled by the party trade union, get a loan from the party credit bureau, read the party newspaper and move in party circles. Breaking party discipline would be for him a very serious thing indeed.

National business was conducted by agreements between party secretariats. Before the state was set up, the Zionist congresses, convening every few years in Europe, acted as a kind of parliament. The congresses were elected only in theory. In many countries, there was no individual membership in the Zionist organization; one became a member automatically by joining a Zionist party. The parties distributed the so-called *shekels*, a Zionist note bearing the name of ancient Hebrew coins and endowing its possessor with the right to vote. Quite often the actual voting would be dispensed with and the number of seats distributed among the parties by common agreement. As the leadership of Zionist parties hardly ever changed (it rarely does even today), the oldtimers knew each other and were used to cooperating, often in complete disregard of the violent denunciations with which they showered each other at election time.

In Palestine itself there grew a power structure controlled by the parties. Sometimes several cooperated in setting up a big instrument, such as the *Histadruth*, the

General Federation of Hebrew Workers; at other times individual parties would create instruments of their own, such as the competing trade unions of the then-Revisionist and Religious Parties. Many of these institutions were consciously equipped with coercive powers. The *Histadruth*, which belonged to the Zionist left-wing parties, controlled the labor exchange, without which it was nearly impossible to find a job. It also had the *Kupath Holim*, the Sick Fund, an admirable institution of medical insurance and service, without which it would have been impossible for an ordinary worker to secure hospitalization and treatment for his family. You could not belong to the Sick Fund without belonging to *Histadruth*. Thus, if the leadership of the workers' parties decided on something, it would become the law of the *Histadruth*. Breaking this law would have meant jeopardizing family, job and medical assistance.

This rigidity was absolutely necessary for policing the state-within-a-state, which had to act quite often against the official British state and its police. Apart from the dissident right-wing Revisionists, everyone agreed that national discipline was absolutely necessary in order to secure the national aims. Of course the dissidents set up their own organization, copying exactly the structure of the official one. As an example of how the system worked, during World War II, the Zionist leadership decided that young Hebrew Palestinians should join the Palestinian units in the British Army to fight the Nazi enemy. This was a voluntary recruitment, and everything was done to ensure that no one failed to volunteer. Young men without a deferment certificate from the National Zionist Recruiting Office found it impossible to get a job, or to receive medical treatment or any other service controlled by the Zionist institutions. Of course, this kind of coercion was secondary; the spirit of purpose, the basic unity and determination of the Hebrew community in Palestine at the time was such that actual coercion was rarely needed. The stigma incurred by anyone not doing the right thing was enough to deter shirkers.

*   *   *

One would think that the state, once established, would have assumed these institutions and functions, with the parties becoming ordinary political groups. But the state machinery was set up by the existing hierarchy, composed of party leaders. The new ministries were staffed by party members, each one of whom owed his job to the party and was loyal to it. The state was superimposed on the party machines; it did not take their place.

The issue of health care is again a good illustration of the pattern. In Israel, everyone agrees that health insurance is essential, that no one should be victimized by disease or accident, that it is the job of society to provide full insurance. (The American attitude in this field is incomprehensible to any Israeli.) It would have been natural, therefore, for a national health service, on the British pattern, to be set up. But health care is controlled by the Sick Funds, which do a good job but are controlled by the parties and give them great leeway for patronage, financial transactions and shady practices. No one (and especially not the socialists) proposes to nationalize health services. As a result, the Ministry of Health does not even try to compete with the Sick Funds. The budget for its operations is much smaller than the budget of the biggest Sick Fund, that run by the *Histadruth*. The primary function of the Ministry is to transfer state money to the non-state Sick Funds, in the form of subsidies and other allocations, making the Sick Funds ever stronger.

The control of education in Israel is also revealing. Before the state was set up, the Hebrew community had created an outstanding system of education, more or less ignoring the governmental Department of Education. All these schools taught the Zionist credo, but were divided into three categories, one general, one socialist, one religious. When the State of Israel was born, this division was officially abandoned for the sake of national unity. In reality, however, a separate religious school system continues within the general public system. It is controlled by the National Religious Party, providing thousands of jobs for its members and tens of thousands of young recruits for its youth organizations. Two smaller religious parties also maintain independent school systems, financed by the government.

One could multiply these examples in every field, except the Army, which is truly national. More than half of the economy belongs to the *Histadruth*, which is not only the biggest trade union, but also the biggest employer in the country. This creates a curious situation in which the chief organization of workers is also the greatest advocate of keeping wages low; thus, the *Histadruth*, a labor federation, has become the main instrument for policing workers and crushing strikes, now mostly wildcat strikes directed as much against the *Histadruth* and the government wage policy as against private employers. In a typical dispute three friends, all members of the same party leadership, meet, one representing the striking workers, one representing the *Histadruth*-owned factory struck, the third a delegate of the government Ministry of Labor.

In the *Histadruth* itself, power is strictly divided, according to a "party key," among the major workers' parties, each providing a proportionate number of its functionaries to staff the *Histadruth* institutions at every level. It is a federation of parties more than a federation of workers.

* * *

Each Zionist party is, thus, a great economic empire.

The left-wing *Mapam* party has dozens of *kibbutzim*, which form an integral part of the party apparatus and finance its elections, institutions and worldwide network of contacts. These *kibbutzim* have an annual turnover of hundreds of millions of Israeli pounds after branching out into industry and many other economic enterprises. They expect the party to see to it that they are liberally provided with government funds and credits, a factor which plays a great role whenever the party is called upon to decide whether or not to join a government coalition.

The National Religious party has two banks and several great economic enterprises, apart from providing many thousands of jobs for rabbis, superintendents of kosher cooking, anti-pig inspectors, and other diverse religious officials, whose salaries are paid by the government, municipal institutions, hotels, shipping lines, and so forth, all the result of the party's continuing success in religious coercion.

The right wing parties control many economic enterprises, generally in a less direct way. But the business interests of all the fringe parties are overshadowed by the economic power of *Mapai*, the dominant force on the political scene since the early Thirties. *Mapai* has managed to concentrate enormous power in all fields of endeavor—from banks and giant corporations right down to the associations of newsstand owners and small tradesmen.

It has been estimated that during the 1965 elections, *Mapai* spent on its campaign more than $50 million, with the other Zionist parties spending proportionate amounts, and even the smallest investing several million—all this in a country whose population is roughly equivalent to that of Brooklyn.

* * *

Not by accident do Zionist parties function as I have described them, nor is it by chance that all are Zionist. In the Zionist past they had to deal with matters which made such machinery necessary. As usual, the machinery continued to flourish and expand long after the need for it had passed. The parties must continue to be Zionist because Zionism provides them with the funds necessary to operate.

Here we come to the crux of the matter—the connection between the Zionist character of the state and the structure of the Establishment. According to the Zionist credo, Israel exists in order to solve the Jewish Question. It is, therefore, only proper that Jews throughout the world should contribute liberally to Israel. To real Zionists, however, the incoming monies are not contributions at all, but a kind of ransom paid by Jews who, contrary to their national duty, do not come to Israel but stick to the fleshpots of the United States and other countries. Monetary contributions are raised in many ways, including the United Jewish Appeal, and flow to Israel in a great stream. In times of war and tension the amount rises, reaching a peak during the 1967 war.

How does this money come to Israel? A great part is

transferred through the Jewish Agency, an anachronism from the days before 1948, when it acted as the Zionist government. The Agency today is an instrument for the distribution of money to the Zionist parties. Unlike the government and Parliament of Israel, over which strict public control is exercised, no real control exists over the Jewish Agency, whose governing bodies are not elected by any normal democratic process. It is a federation of party secretariats, pure and simple, a system for the division of the spoils. Several million dollars are parceled out directly among the Zionist parties, ostensibly as compensation for relinquishing their rights to organize their own fund-raising in the United States. But this represents only a fraction of the real division; by financing youth organizations, educational activities, propaganda agencies, and other institutions belonging to the Zionist parties, the Jewish Agency goes a long way toward sustaining the huge apparatus every Zionist party maintains in Israel and abroad. But even this is not its most important function. By agreement between the State of Israel and the Zionist organization, the State has abdicated to the organization its role in organizing immigration, absorbing the immigrants, setting up new agricultural settlements and supporting the old ones. These immense operations are conducted, even today in Israel, by the Jewish Agency.

Thus parties controlling the Zionist organization can manipulate vast amounts of money independent of ordinary democratic processes and controls. Small wonder indeed that to all these parties Zionism is sacred. The Establishment could not possibly exist without it. The idea of a non-Zionist Israel is to them heresy, mortal sin.

*   *   *

The relationship between the parties and the government is not very different, even while subject to far stricter controls.

The Israeli economy, for example, is run as few others. It is a system which, in my view, resembles neither capitalism nor socialism, but is a unique creation. No general plan exists, as in a planned socialist economy, nor is there private initiative, as in an advanced capitalistic society. Instead, the government exerts absolute power over all economic activity by a very sophisticated system of controlled credit, permits, licenses, quotas, subsidies, taxation, currency control, and so forth, without any central planning board; no such board exists. Many people got rich in Israel, but not one without the government's wanting him to. Private entrepreneurs, especially Jews from abroad, can win incredible conditions for new enterprises. In some notorious cases, charlatans received from the government, in grants and loans, much more than the entire amount invested in the enterprises. But every activity is dependent upon some government support or intervention, given or withheld without objective rules, and without recourse to appeal.

There is an explanation for this capricious system. During the first years of the state, great amounts of money were poured into it through one door, while hundreds of thousands of immigrants were pouring in through another. Jobs had to be provided quickly. Factories were set up indiscriminately, generally without much attention to their profit potential. While some investments have proved sound, others have not. Great parts of the economy are continually dependent on new subsidies administered by the government, thus giving the government decisive economic powers.

The political parties, controlling the government, participate in this power, with *Mapai* retaining the lion's share but all the others getting a part of it. If a party is well organized, it will use the benefits it receives from the government, the Jewish Agency, the municipalities, and the *Histadruth*, as well as the profits of its own economic enterprises, in order to gain votes by well-financed propaganda and the provision of jobs. If it wins an election victory, which means gaining a few additional seats in parliament, it may trade in this gain for new economic benefits when the new government coalition is formed. Another circle.

At the center of power stands *Mapai*, controlling the important ministries in the government and the other key posts in the state from the President of Israel to the general secretary of the *Histadruth*, and the mayors of all important cities. With little more than a third of the vote, it was in complete control of political life, even before it was rejoined by the *Rafi* and *Achdut-Haavada* parties and became the Israel Labor Party in January 1968. No one could possibly become Prime Minister without being nominated by the *Mapai* Secretariat. Moshe Dayan, therefore, had no chance at all to succeed Eshkol before he rejoined the *Mapai* party. He knew this well, which explains his ardent support for the return of the *Rafi* party to its mother's lap, even against the violent opposition of his former mentor, Ben-Gurion. No one could have guaranteed Dayan the position of heir apparent even after *Rafi* had rejoined *Mapai*, for *Mapai* basically is a vast union of office-holders, big and small, from cabinet ministers to local labor exchange chiefs. There are no clear-cut permanent factions within the party; groups align themselves according to passing interests. Decisions are reached by a vague, ill-defined process, filtering through many institutions, until some kind of consensus is found. In this climate, a man like the Minister of Finance, Pinchas Sapir, has by far more chance to succeed Eshkol than a lone wolf like Dayan.

* * *

This, then, is the Establishment, uniting ideology with vested interest, Zionist dogma with party finances, heartfelt beliefs with patronage—and rarely is there a clear dividing line. The Establishment has withstood the winds of change, even as a community of just over half a million became a sovereign state of more than two and a half million, with all the trappings of modern statehood.

For anyone who believes in the necessity of deep structural change in order to ensure the future of Israel, this could be a very pessimistic picture. Indeed, only three years ago it was an axiom in Israel that no new political force had even a ghost of a chance to raise its head. Yet, as Ilya Ehrenburg has said, "You could cover the whole world with asphalt, but sooner or later green grass would break through." The Establishment, while extremely powerful, long ago lost real contact with the people, especially with the younger generation. Its inability to solve the real problems of the country, and especially the Arab problem, has become obvious. The decay of Zionism is making the Establishment obsolete.

The first blade of grass peeping through the asphalt is the new party to which I belong. During the 1965 elections, something happened which was considered impossible even the day before: for the first time since the Twenties, a different political outlook met the test of election. The new party, called the New Force (or the *Ha'olam Hazeh* Movement, because it was initiated by the magazine which bears this name), received 1.2 per cent of the vote, evenly dispersed throughout the country, but with a much higher percentage in the army, some frontier settlements and the Israeli Arabs. It is a small victory, but of significance. It was also a cheap victory. While other parties spent tens of millions of Israeli pounds in a vast orgy of waste, the New Force spent about forty thousand—and certainly could neither promise nor provide jobs or benefits to anyone.

More significantly, the New Force is non-Zionist, and its leaders have been ostracized for many years for advocating such heretical ideas as a return of the Arab refugees, cooperation with Arab nationalism, and abolishing the Zionist organization. Yet thousands of voters throughout the country, especially in the younger generation, the *kibbutzim* and the army, openly supported this new movement. The New Force also advocates that Israel should cease to declare itself a Jewish state, but rather become a pluralist one. It believes in full equality of the Israeli Arabs, in a complete separation of synagogue and state, and for promulgation of a written constitution, still sadly lacking in Israel after twenty years.

Israel has a long way to go before a real change will be effected, enabling the country to assume a new posture in the Region. Yet, our initial success proves, at long last, that new forces can arise in Israel, that the winds of change are blowing stronger, and that conditions are ripening which may create the psychological and political prerequisite for breaking the vicious circle —finding a solution to the Arab-Israeli conflict.

11: *The Federation of Palestine*

THE WAR between Israel and the Arab world is not an ordinary one between states. In an ordinary war states clash over some grievance, a piece of land or economic advantages. After the war, some kind of peace arrangements are made, tracing new boundaries or allocating rights, sometimes by agreement, sometimes by dictate of the victor. Ours is a different war, a clash between two great national movements going on now for three generations. It cannot be ended by a peace settlement of the classic type, with representatives of the two sides assembling in conference around a green table, each party stating its demands, a compromise hammered out and embodied in a solemn peace treaty.

Many concrete problems are bones of contention between Israel and the Arabs, yet not one of them constitutes the real cause of the war. While solutions to these problems must be found, as we shall endeavor to do, one must realize that no solution will be practical unless the genuine causes of the war are removed. Quite simply: Israel must recognize that it belongs to the Region and must take a positive attitude toward the national aspirations of the Arab peoples. The Arab world must recognize that Israel exists and has become a legal and permanent part of the Region.

This mutual recognition is the focal point of the problem. Without it, all talks about a Regional peace settlement are nonsense. Without it, all foreign intervention and attempts at mediation, well intentioned or otherwise, will be of no avail. Mediators, go-betweens, peace brokers may be important as messengers in certain phases, but they are no substitute for direct confrontation between Israel and the Arabs.

*   *   *

Which Arabs?

This important question is often overlooked. The answer, to my mind, is, first of all, the Arab-Palestinian nation.

One unresolved question in the Middle East is whether the Arabs constitute one nation or a group of nations. In other words, whether all the Arabs can or should unite in one big Arab state, stretching from the shores of Morocco to the boundaries of Iran, or whether they should retain the separate existing states. The idea of unity is inherent in the Arab national movement. Arabs look back with longing at the time, glorious but short-lived, when the whole Arab world, indeed all of Islam, was united under the caliph. In modern times both the Baath ("resurrection") party, centered in Syria, and Abd-el-Nasser have been spokesmen for the idea of the great unitary Arab state. Yet it seems this idea has failed. As in Europe and Africa, and even in the Soviet bloc, smaller states stick to their own political existence and interests, even while recognizing a broader, unifying regional idea.

Each Arab people has its own state, save one: the people of Palestine. This people was the great loser of the 1948 war. According to the original United Nations partition resolution of November 29, 1947, an independent Arab state was to be set up in those parts of Palestine which were not allocated to the Jewish state. Such an Arab state never came about. The war, which the Arabs of Palestine themselves started in order to prevent the partition of the country and the establishment of Israel, created new realities. During the war, which Israel did not want, Israel conquered part of the areas originally allocated to the Arabs. The neighboring Arab states, which sent their armies into Palestine in order to help their brethren, ultimately annexed the remaining parts of Palestine. At the end of the war Palestine had ceased to exist as a political entity; it was divided among Israel, Egypt and Jordan. Yet Palestine remained a mental reality. The Palestinians never resigned themselves to a fate which meant that they had ceased to exist as a nation. In Jordan, in the Gaza Strip, in refugee camps dispersed all over the Region, the idea of Palestine lived on. It was exploited by the Arab states in their fight against Israel and among themselves, each of several states trying to usurp the role of the patron of the Palestinian nation. Egypt installed a shadowy adventurer, Ahmed Shukairy, a refugee from Haifa, as the chief of the Palestine Liberation Organization, a post he was forced to relinquish in December 1967. Hussein pretended that his shaky kingdom was the true personification of Palestine. The Syrians supported the Palestinian *el Fatah* ("conquest") organiza-

tion, whose acts of sabotage led directly to the crisis of
the 1967 war.

The official Israeli attitude has fluctuated between
diametrically opposed poles, according to expediency.
Until the 1948 war, the Zionist leadership insisted that
its conflict was solely with the Palestinian Arabs. It
objected vigorously to the official invitation extended
by the British government to the Arab states to take
part in discussing the Palestine problem. This was believed to be a typical trick of perfidious Albion, an
attempt to cheat us out of our rights and annul the
Balfour Declaration. After the 1948 war, the government of Israel maintained that Palestine had ceased to
exist, together with any imaginary Palestinian nation,
and that its conflict was now solely with the Arab
states. This stand was taken because any recognition of
the existence of a Palestinian nation might raise questions about boundaries and refugees which the government was anxious to avoid. Now, after the 1967 war,
the situation has changed again. Except for some hundreds of thousands of former and new refugees, all
Arab Palestinians live in the territories occupied by the
Israeli Army during this war, and these territories include all the area of Palestine as it existed under the
British Mandate until 1948.

The question of what to do with these territories is,
therefore, bound up with the question whether to recognize the Palestinian-Arab nation and deal with it or
disregard its existence.

* * *

Today the Israeli government insists that the present
situation—the precarious cease-fire—can be changed
only if the Arab governments start direct and open

negotiations with Israel. Moreover, the Israeli government refuses to state, or even to hint, what its condition for peace may be. It says that only during the official, direct negotiations with the Arab governments will it state these conditions.

This very comfortable and expedient stand relieves the Israeli government of the necessity to decide upon peace-conditions, a task quite beyond the present Great Coalition, some of whose members could not agree to anything but full and outright annexation, while some of its other members could not tolerate annexation. Premier Eshkol who, like President Johnson, wants to be the personification of a great consensus, would like to keep this coalition intact until the elections of 1969, thereby postponing a move in any direction.

For the Arab states, direct negotiations as a *first* step are impossible. Such a repudiation of all the slogans which dominated the Arab world for fifty years cannot be the beginning of the road to peace, but rather the end of it. Many things—the solution of the Palestinian refugee problem, the neutralization of many other factors which poison the region—must come first.

Moreover, the Arab governments suspect that the call for direct negotiations is a trap. As a high-ranking Egyptian official put it to me: "What does Israel want from us? Only recognition of its lawful existence. We, on our part, have many concrete demands—retreat from the cease-fire lines, repatriation of refugees, and so forth. If we agree to direct peace negotiations, we already do accord Israel recognition. In other words, we are giving you *in advance* what you want, without receiving anything in return. After making such a mistake, Israel could say, at the negotiating table, that it does not want to concede anything. Therefore, secret negotiations by mediators must come first. We must know what Israel wants to give up in return for recognition, before any Arab leader can make any open move."

Thus a new vicious circle is formed—one which allows the Israeli and Arab governments to postpone everything.

This postponement is also freezing debate in Israel itself, with the unfortunate result that no one knows where public opinion really stands. The struggle between the adherents of annexation and federation cuts across nearly all the parties. The propagandists for a Greater Israel are more vociferous, and command much more support in the mass-circulation press, but the adherents of a Palestinian federation are far more numerous and influential than would seem at first glance. Significantly, many of them belong to the higher echelons of the Israeli Army which, quite unlike most armies, is one of the least chauvinistic and most sober factors on the Israeli scene. The military governors who administer the occupied territories of Palestine, as well as many higher civilian government officials, in general advocate a more liberal and farsighted policy than many politicians and publicists.

A few weeks ago, I proposed in the *Knesset* a resolution calling for immediate steps to create a Palestinian Republic. The first paragraph read: "The whole of Palestine is the homeland of two nations—the Hebrew nation and the Arab-Palestinian nation." I proposed that two states embodying the two nations—Israel and the Republic of Palestine—should form a federation.

Only one other member voted for this resolution. But after the vote, twelve members, ranging from the right-wing *Herut* to the left-wing *Mapam*, and including a cabinet minister, approached me privately in the lobby, expressing their private support, adding wistfully: "I wish I could have voted for this resolution." By Israeli standards of party discipline, this was, of course, impossible, as all the great parties support the government policy of waiting for direct negotiations with the Arab states.

In a famous remark, Moshe Dayan has said that he is "waiting for the Arab leaders to ring his telephone." This is now official Israeli policy. The point is that this policy is aimed only at negotiations with *existing* Arab governments—and thus excludes automatically the one Arab people which has as yet no government, but who is the most directly concerned—the Palestinian people, with whom a solution can be worked out and implemented at once.

* * *

In fact, three alternatives face Israel today, after the 1967 war.

The first is to give the occupied territories back to the neighboring Arab states. Very few Israelis think that that is either practical or desirable. At worst, it would mean that hostile Arab armies would appear again sooner or later in their old positions, ten miles from the seashore of Nathanya, fifteen miles from the heart of Tel Aviv, with future wars virtually inevitable. At best, if the Arab states do agree to some kind of peaceful settlement, it would mean that Israel would still be surrounded by the dispossessed Palestinian Arabs, longing for their own national identity, a cause for further trouble. The question of Jerusalem, now unified and annexed by Israel and the focus of intense emotions on both sides, makes such a solution even more unlikely.

The second, opposite proposal, shrilly demanded by a coalition of all the more extreme elements in Israel, would be the annexation of all or most of the occupied territories. Here, two inherent traits of Zionism clash. As a colonizing movement, Zionism is expansionist by nature, at least within the historical boundaries of Palestine. It is, therefore, quite natural for an old-time Zionist to advocate the "liberation" of all of Palestine, opening up new areas for Jewish settlement. Yet this instinctive demand, quite natural after a victorious war, clashes with another inherent trait of Zionism: the idea of a homogeneous Jewish state. Israel has not succeeded in integrating 300,000 Israeli Arabs into its psychological structure; how, then, could it absorb nearly a million and a half? The annexation of the territories and their inhabitants would turn Israel into a bi-national state, an idea detested by most Israelis. Worse, the natural increase of Palestinian Arabs being more than two times greater than that of Hebrew Israelis (45 as against 22 per thousand) and no significant Jewish immigration in sight, it seems virtually certain that the Arabs would be the majority in Greater Israel within less than a generation, thereby achieving the very aim they set themselves before the creation of Israel—a Palestinian state ruled by an Arab majority, who could stop immigration. There may be some on the lunatic fringe of the annexation idea who believe the Arabs should and could be evicted in due course from the country, enabling all of Palestine to become a homogeneous state. Others advocate that these Arabs should not be given citizenship rights after annexation, thus turning Israel into a new South Africa or Rhodesia, with the Hebrew citizens exercising political power over a native population in the minority today but perhaps the majority tomorrow. Several politicians of the old parties have advocated a policy to "help and encourage" Arabs to emigrate from Palestine.

Annexation means turning Israel into a Hebrew empire, with a colonial regime controlling the Arab inhabitants. No one can believe that within such an empire, plagued with an ever-growing problem of inner security and armed resistance, democracy could be preserved even for Hebrew citizens—emergency laws and arbitrary rule have a way of expanding, once applied on a large scale. One way or another, annexation would be the end of Israel as we know it, the end of any hope for peaceful integration in the Region, the final turning of Israel into an armed Crusader state.

This is not only true about outright, official annexation. The status quo may generate another kind of annexation—a creeping, unannounced, factual annexation, brought about by hundreds of little acts and omissions. Here a Hebrew settlement is set up, temporarily, to support the army of occupation, there an abandoned Arab village is razed to the ground for "security and sanitary reasons" (as Moshe Dayan said the other day in the *Knesset*, in answer to my question). If such acts accumulate, a point of no return may be reached, which will have the same results as an official annexation. Practical annexation might become the continuation of old-time "practical" Zionism.

The third alternative is to encourage the setting up of an Arab republic of Palestine. My friends and I have advocated this plan for Israel's integration into the Semitic Region since 1948, long before the Six-Day

War and the occupation of the West Bank and the Gaza Strip.

In the present circumstances, it would mean that the government of Israel would offer the Palestinian Arabs assistance in setting up a national republic of their own, this offer being conditional upon a federal agreement between such a Palestine and Israel. The Palestinian Republic would comprise the west bank of the Jordan and the Gaza Strip. Transjordan could join it if its inhabitants were able and willing so to decide.

Jerusalem as a unified city would become the federal capital, as well as the capital of both states, thus finding a solution—the only practical one, I believe—to an issue charged with emotions, both religious and nationalist, which make retreat for either side impossible.

The federal agreement should be preceded by an economic, political and military pact. It should safeguard the military security of Israel by forbidding foreign armies to enter the territory of Palestine, guaranteeing this in a practical way by a system of military coordination between the armies of Israel and the Arab republic of Palestine on the lines of NATO or the Warsaw Pact. It should unify the economy of the area, which had been one economic entity from the dawn of history to 1948, including the two hundred years of the Crusader State. It should establish some form of political coordination, providing, for example, that neither Israel nor Palestine should enter any foreign alliance without the agreement of the other. This is the bare minimum, which could be expanded, gradually and by mutual consent, into a deeper and more significant federation, once Arab Palestine catches up, economically and socially, with Israel.

Such, then, is the plan which the government of Israel should offer the Palestinian-Arab nation, those residing in the territories now occupied by the Israeli Army and those outside, who must be allowed to return.

Many doubts and objections have been raised to this plan. Some of my Arab friends fear that such a Palestinian republic would be free in name only, becoming in reality a kind of Bantustan, like the so-called "autonomous" Negro reservations set up by the racist white regime in South Africa. This danger would exist if the plan were used by an anti-Arab regime in Israel as a camouflage for what would really be colonialist expansion. But every plan can be perverted, and this possibility is no argument against it. The plan as such, executed in the same spirit in which it is offered, should be the subject of debate. The real question is: Can the Palestinian republic become a living organism, a more or less equal partner with Israel?

I answer the question in the affirmative. True, after twenty years of Jordanian and Egyptian rule, both the Gaza Strip and the West Bank are devoid of any industry. Just now, they are no match for Israel in this sphere. But things have to be viewed in a more dynamic context. The settlement of the refugees and the restoration of the Arab territories to their natural place in a unified country will give their economy a boost on the road to economic prosperity. Politically, the very fact that this will be an Arab republic, a part of the Arab world with which Israel has to deal, will give the Palestinian republic a status of importance beyond its own resources. It will become the natural bridge between Israel and the Arab world.

This idea of a bridge is central to our concept. We don't want a quisling state, serving Israel and considered as treasonous by the other Arab peoples. On the contrary, the Republic of Palestine, in order to fulfill its natural function as a bridge of peace, must be a true expression of the Palestinian nationality, led by true leaders, and acceptable to the Arab world.

We do not conceive the Palestinian solution as opposed to a regional settlement—but rather as a step toward it, and eventually as a part of it. Even today, the products of the West Bank, mainly agricultural, daily cross the Jordan bridges and fords, on their way to Transjordan, Kuwait, even Iraq and Saudi Arabia. Many Palestinians travel from the occupied territory to Transjordan and back, to conduct their business. Thus, owing to the situation of the Palestinian Arabs, the cease-fire lines are not as hermetically closed as the old armistice lines, which were crossed only by terrorists, soldiers and smugglers. Palestine already serves as a bridge.

If Israel offers the Palestinian nation assistance in setting up their republic, and if this offer is accepted by a responsible Palestinian leadership, one of the first moves should be for these leaders to go to Cairo and other Arab capitals, in order to canvass overall Arab support for this solution. My judgment is that Egypt and its allies—while not openly welcoming this plan—will make it clear that they do not object to it. Indeed, in one of his most extreme anti-Israeli speeches at the end of 1967, Gamal Abd-el-Nasser still emphasized that the Palestinian question is a matter for the Palestinians themselves to solve, and that from them must come the initiative for a settlement. This was interpreted by many Palestinian leaders as a green light to go ahead—cautiously.

But—some Zionists ask—are the Palestinians a nation? After all, there never existed an independent Arab state of Palestine. What right have the Palestinians to a state of their own?

There is a certain irony in the fact that these questions are raised by Zionists—for not long ago these same arguments were thrown into their own faces. Were the Jews a nation? Was even the Hebrew community in Palestine a real nation, deserving statehood? I remember that these same questions were raised by French propagandists and generals during the Algerian war of liberation, which I supported. I was often told by Frenchmen in Paris that there just does not exist an Algerian nation, that there never existed a united Algerian-Arab state.

The answer for the Palestinians, as it was for the Hebrews and the Algerians, is: people who believe that they are a nation, thereby do become a nation. This is the only valid criterion. Once a people aspires to statehood, longs for it and strives for it, they deserve it. Whether this state ever existed before, whether it has a history or not, is quite immaterial. Even today the Palestinian nation is stronger than many of the nations in the United Nations.

The merits of Palestinian-Arab statehood are not a debating point in New York or Paris. It is in Nablus, Ramallah and Gaza that it has to stand its test. No one who visits these towns, who speaks freely with their inhabitants, can fail to be impressed by the intensity of Palestinian nationalism, by the deep conviction of people of all ages who answer clearly: We are not Jordanians, nor Egyptians. We are Palestinians. *Filasteen* is our country. As Palestinians we are part of the Arab world.

I believe in the force of nationalism as a prime

mover in contemporary history. Try to combat nationalism, and you are bound to lose. Harness nationalism to concrete solutions of problems, and you have a chance to put an end to war. If we try to suppress this nationalism, we only create a vacuum which will be filled by adventurers like the detested Shukairy, or by terrorists like the *al-Fatah*, who are trying to start a genuine war of liberation against Israel. Nature abhors a vacuum. Wishing Palestine away will not make it disappear. Like the ghost of Hamlet's father, it will haunt the Region and Israel, creating new dangers and new miseries.

But once a provisional Palestinian Government is formed, once the black, white and green colors of Palestine are unfurled side by side with the blue and white flag of Israel, a real revolution will be set in motion, a revolution which will change the climate of the whole Region.

For Israel, it will mean the beginning of peace, actual cooperation between it and an authentic Arab state. For the Palestinian nation, it will mean an end to frustration, a place on the map, the restoration of its national identity, a safeguard to its territorial integrity, and, last but not least, an end to the misery of the refugees.

12: Samson's Foxes
and the Refugees

It is to the refugee question that we must now address ourselves. No problem in the Region is more loaded with hatred and bitterness, fear and anxiety, than this one. To the Arabs, the refugees are a tragedy, a constant reminder of failure and humiliation, a living memory of an injustice done and not redressed. To Israel, the refugees are a constant danger, a reservoir of tomorrow's terrorists, and worse, the nightmare of a potential advancing flood which would submerge the State of Israel, set up by so much sacrifice.

There is not much use in analyzing the causes of this tragedy. Yet there seems no way of avoiding it. The propaganda of both sides, based on half-truths and deliberate falsehoods, has poisoned the atmosphere of the Region for too long. How, then, did these Arabs become refugees? Were they driven out by cruel Israeli invaders who took over their country, as Arab propaganda maintains, or did they flee on the advice of their leaders, hoping to return in a few days after the massacre of the Jews by the Arab armies, as Israeli propaganda proclaims?

* * *

On a recent visit to the huge refugee camp near Gaza, I asked an Arab boy, "Where do you come from?" He answered, "From al-Koubab."

I was struck by this answer for two reasons: first, because he was a boy of seven and, therefore, born at Gaza, twelve years after his family had left Israeli territory, and he has never seen al-Koubab, a village which ceased to exist long ago, its pitiful houses leveled by bulldozers preparing the land for a new settlement. Secondly, because I had personal memories of al-Koubab. As a soldier of Samson's Foxes I had taken part in the capture of the village. We had surrounded it in the night, after firing a few rounds of ammunition. Upon entering the abandoned houses, we found ovens that were still hot, and dishes on the table. Some hundreds of persons had gone to swell the ranks of the refugees.

I took part in many operations of this kind, which I cannot but recall when the problem of the refugees comes up. I believe, therefore, that I am as qualified as anyone to give an objective account of what actually happened.

The first fact to take into consideration is that the 1948 war was not a war between regular armies of normal states. The rules of civilized warfare did not apply. It was, rather, a violent collision between two movements of almost religious fervor—one, colonizing Zionism; the other, xenophobic nationalism. Each sought to destroy the other. This kind of war degenerates easily into a battle of extermination.

The fighting may be roughly divided into three main

phases. During each of these, people left their homes and became refugees for quite different reasons.

The first began on November 30, 1947, only a few hours after the General Assembly of the U.N. had adopted the partition plan. This phase was to last until the end of March 1948. During this period, the war was conducted on the Arab side by irregulars and primitive villagers, who killed and multilated every Hebrew who fell into their hands. We all saw the pictures of the severed heads of our comrades paraded through the alleys of the Old City of Jerusalem, of unrecognizable corpses with their sexual organs stuffed into their mouths. No one can quite understand what happened later on without realizing the impact of these pictures on the small Hebrew community, then comprising less than 650,000 people, faced with virtual extermination.

During this phase certain numbers of Arabs fled from their homes in urban quarters and villages that happened to be close to the Hebrew strongholds. They often did so without being attacked or conquered, apparently on the orders of regional commanders. In certain cases, the *Haganah* Army, endangering the lives of its soldiers, distributed leaflets in Arab villages calling upon the inhabitants not to leave. To understand this, it is necessary to remember that the Arabs, the British and the U.S. State Department were all trying to demonstrate to the world that the partition plan was not workable and that a U.N. trusteeship for Palestine was the only solution. Throughout the spring of 1948, the State Department and the U.S. military leaders tried to supersede the partition plan with a new plan of U.N. trusteeship. James Forrestal, the first Secretary of Defense of the United States, who fought vigorously against the establishment of Israel, wrote in his diary,

on March 29, 1948, that he asked President Truman to
commit American troops to Palestine in order to en-
force a trusteeship plan—against the Hebrew Army, of
course. The President did not want to make such a
commitment, but the editor of the Forrestal diary
comments that "American policy had now shifted to
the advocacy of a joint Anglo-French-American trusteeship, which [Warren R.] Austin was about to
present to the United Nations."

One of the prime movers of the idea was Dean Rusk,
then director of the State Department's Office of Political Affairs. "If we did nothing," Rusk said, according
to the Forrestal diary, "it was likely that the Russians
could and would take definite steps toward gaining control in Palestine through the infiltration of specially
trained [Jewish] immigrants, or by otherwise capitaliz-
ing on the widespread, violent civil war that would be
likely to break out." Rusk believed that this might in-
volve the slaughter of "perhaps hundreds of thousands."

In the face of this conspiracy against the partition
plan, it was of the utmost importance for the Zionist
leadership to prove not only that the Hebrew Army
could control the situation, but also that the more than
half a million Arabs, living in the part of Palestine
allocated to the Hebrew state, could well live there
happily forever, and, therefore, that the partition plan
was both workable and humane. It is certain that the
Zionist leadership did not plan or encourage the flight
of the Arabs at that time.

The second phase lasted until mid-May, 1948. The
armies on both sides were reinforced. The Arabs rallied
round regional military leaders, who established some
kind of organization. The *Haganah* Army became a

regular fighting force, executing detailed military plans. The fighting took place mainly on the roads linking the pockets of Hebrew colonization, and in the course of it, a more or less continuous area held by the *Haganah* was created. It was during this phase that most of the larger towns passed into the hands of the Hebrew Army. At this time, conflicting policies seem to have been entertained by the Zionist leaders. Possibly some had come to the conclusion that the massive exodus of the Arabs might be a good thing. Yet some Jewish leaders tried to persuade Arabs to remain in a captured area, for example, in Haifa. However, generally, it seems the Arabs were encouraged to evacuate their towns and villages, both by their own leaders and by the Hebrew Army.

It was during this period, at dawn on April 10, 1948, that the notorious massacre of Deir-Yassin took place. This small Arab village near Jerusalem was occupied, after a night battle, by a unit of the *Irgun*. (The *Irgun* forces, already in the process of being absorbed by the *Haganah* Army, were then operating under the general command of the *Haganah*.) All the inhabitants of the village who had not fled—men, women and children— were massacred. The impact of this carnage on the Arab population of Palestine was immense and accelerated the flight of villagers in other areas of the country. Later, I tried to interrogate the soldiers who took part in the action. They maintained that the massacre was not premeditated, that their local commander lost his head after some of his men were killed by Arab snipers. But while Deir-Yassin became a symbol, it was by no means an isolated incident. Killings of this nature had been perpetrated by both sides previously and many more took place subsequently. After the indiscriminate killing of Hebrews by Arabs at the beginning of the war, the civilians of both sides expected to be annihilated if they fell into enemy hands.

In the course of a scientific conference in 1957, General Yigal Allon, who had been in command of operations in the north during that phase, said, rather delicately, "While planning the capture of the Arab part of Safed, it was not our intention to prevent the flight of the Arab population." Moreover, the historical department of the Israeli Army has published battle plans which show that during that phase, the combat brigades had orders to push the Arab population out of certain parts of the country, in order to establish defensive areas in preparation for the expected invasion of the Arab armies.

The third phase started with this invasion on May 15, and lasted until the end of the war in 1949. The regular armies of Egypt, Jordan, Syria, Iraq and Lebanon invaded the territory that had been Palestine, with the express intent of liquidating the Hebrew state newly created. They faced the *Haganah* Army which became, in June, officially the Israel Defense Army (a name which allowed for the inclusion of the word *Haganah*, meaning defense). The fighting was interrupted several times by cease-fires orders of the United Nations, which were conveniently ignored whenever one side thought it could gain an advantage thereby.

I believe that during this phase, the eviction of Arab civilians had become an aim of David Ben-Gurion and his government. After the United Nations had failed so miserably in implementing the partition plan, and the State of Israel had been set up by the sole force of Israeli arms, U.N. opinion could very well be disregarded. Peace with the Arabs seemed out of the question, considering the extreme nature of the Arab propaganda. In this situation, it was easy for people like Ben-Gurion to believe that the capture of uninhabited territory was both necessary for security reasons and desirable for the homogeneity of the new Hebrew state.

How was this objective attained? During this phase of the fighting, real massacres were rare on both sides. Generally, it was sufficient to fire a few rounds into an Arab village to make the inhabitants, who had not fought in a war for generations, take flight. According to Zionist propaganda, the Arab governments and the Arab armies called upon the Arabs to leave their homes. Unfortunately, this has never been proved. Erskine Childers, a serious, if pro-Arab writer, has assured me that he went over all the monitored broadcasts of the Arab stations during 1948, copies of which are preserved by the BBC in London, but did not find a single order, or even suggestion, pointing in this direction. On the contrary, it seems that the Arab governments asked the inhabitants not to leave. I am inclined to believe that while local Arab leaders in the first stage of the war requested the Arabs to evacuate their homes rather than stay behind in Israeli-held territory, a different attitude was taken by the Arab governments in the third stage of the war. The exact opposite happened in each phase on the Israeli side.

But even this analysis misses the real point. The main exodus of the Arabs was not at all the result of premeditated policies, of either the Arabs or of the Zionists, but rather a natural result of the war as such. Few people realize nowadays that the Arabs never fled the country. Actually, when an Arab fighting unit retreated from one village to the next, during an Israeli advance, the population of the abandoned village retreated with the troops, fearing the worst. Israelis often say that the Arabs were afraid because they knew what they would have done to Israelis if the situations had been reversed; the truth is that it is natural for primitive people to abandon their homes for a few days while their village is under attack. If the Israeli *kibbutzniks* and other villagers did not do this, but stayed on and fought with the army to the very last, it was because of the unique character of these defense-minded villages—and the general feeling of all Israelis during the war that there was No Alternative, nowhere to go, that we had to stand and fight whatever the outcome might be. No Alternative—*ein brera* in Hebrew—was the slogan of the war, a way of thinking, a common resolve every individual in the new state held intensely during that crucial war.

Arab civilians were thus progressively pushed back, a few miles at a time, gradually getting farther and farther from their homes, but always believing that return was only a matter of days or weeks. When the armistice was signed, they suddenly found an international frontier standing between them and their homes. They had become refugees.

Only the Arabs who lived in areas overrun by the Israeli Army in lightning campaigns, when there was no time to flee (and when the Israeli Army was not interested in having the roads blocked by refugees) remained in Israel. This was the case in Nazareth and the whole of Galilee. To this were added the Arabs living in a string of villages ceded by Jordan under the armistice agreement, after the fighting had come to an end.

* * *

For my part I think it is futile to try to fix the initial responsibility for the refugee tragedy on one side or the other. The exodus was inevitable, much as the war itself had been made inevitable by the operation of the vicious circle. Such responsibility as there is must be shared by both sides. Cowardice, irresponsibility and indifference, were as responsible as terrorization, lack of humanity, and the brute spirit of violence.

On the Arab side, no constructive war aim had been formulated throughout the war or, indeed, until today. The victory of the Arabs in 1948 would have meant a national disaster for the Israelis, a second Holocaust, possibly total physical extermination. On the Israeli side, the colonizing spirit inherent in Zionism was well-served by the flight of the Arabs, which left thousands of houses and hundreds of thousands of acres owner-less, to be turned over to the hundreds of thousands of Jewish immigrants pouring into the country after 1948. Because of the immigration, it was anathema to Israelis even to think about the possibility of repatriation.

Many reasons have been advanced to justify the Is-raeli stand—legalistic, economic and political, and the overriding considerations of internal security. Each has some validity, but could also be refuted. The average Israeli quite sincerely believes that giving the refugees the right to return would mean a catastrophic flood of hatred-ridden Arabs submerging the new state by force of numbers. Personally, I believe that behind all the arguments against repatriation, plausible and senseless, there lies the basic ideal of Zionism: a homogeneous Jewish state, a state "as Jewish as England is English," as was said many times by Zionist leaders.

My friends and I have advocated, since the very first days after the '48 war, the principle of giving the refugees the choice between repatriation and compensation. While compensation without repatriation has been offered by the Israeli Government, but was unacceptable to the Arabs, any kind of repatriation is by far the most unpopular view anyone can propagate in Israel. Yet we feel that the solution of the refugee problem is the key to peace, an act of reconciliation between Israel and the Palestinian-Arab nation which should be the beginning rather than the result of peace in the Region. We offered a detailed plan based on the following principles:

1) Israel recognizes the principle of the right of the Arab refugees to return to Israeli territory.

2) Every refugee should be asked, as an individual, to make a free choice between repatriation and compensation.

3) The refugees opting for return will be repatriated over a period of ten years under an annual quota, each year a tenth returning.

4) The repatriates would be settled and provided with new means of livelihood in the cities and villages, much as Jewish immigrants are. (The refugees could not be returned to their former individual homes, most of which have long ceased to exist, without dislocating hundreds of thousands of citizens and upsetting the whole economy of the country.)

5) Returning refugees would automatically become Israeli citizens, enjoying all civil rights.

6) Compensation, to those relinquishing the right to return, would be according to a scale fixed in advance. Payments would be in hard currency, and would cover abandoned property, as well as loss of livelihood, education, and so forth.

7) The cost of resettlement and compensation would be financed by international funds.

8) The whole scheme would be a unilateral Israeli operation, without foreign interference, and not conditional on any political settlement.

9) The Arab refugees would be invited to set up a representative body to cooperate with Israel in the realization of this plan.

We expected that under such a scheme, many of the refugees, probably the majority, would opt for compensation and settlement in the Arab world, with the minority opting for return. It was a practical and ideal solution, the best which could be realistically proposed in the circumstances prevailing until June 1967. The Six-Day War has changed these circumstances completely—both for better and for worse.

* * *

This war created a new refugee problem. While hundreds of thousands of the refugees of 1948 have stayed in their camps in territory captured by the Israeli Army with lightning speed during the six fateful days of June 1967, about 250,000 Palestinians crossed into Transjordan to become refugees there, and a slightly smaller number of Syrians fled from the narrow strip occupied by the Israeli Army on the Syrian plateau.

Again analysis is difficult. As no one in Israel had actually foreseen the entry of Jordan into the war, there did not exist any clear-cut plan about what to do with the inhabitants of the captured territory during the military operations and immediately afterwards. In the absence of such a plan, local commanders acted on their own in different ways; some of them, perhaps in-

fluenced by Defense Minister Dayan, seem to have encouraged a new Arab exodus. Many Arabs left volun-
tarily. Lack of economic opportunity on the West
Bank, and even more so in the Gaza Strip, which have
been treated shabbily by the Jordanian and Egyptian
authorities, has induced an incredible number of young
men and women to find employment in Kuwait, Saudi
Arabia and Algeria. These people used to send part of
their salaries back to their families, for most the only
source of income. When families found themselves
within Israeli-occupied territory, they feared, naturally,
that their remittances from the Arab countries would be
cut off. They hastened to cross into Transjordan while
the road was still open. Another refugee contingent
seems to be composed of many of the old 1948 group
who had lived in camps on the West Bank and were
pushed by Israeli commanders over the bridges into
Jordan. Some thousands were summarily evicted from
the town of Kalkilia and several villages in the Latrun
area of the West Bank when someone decided, without
government approval, to destroy these townships for
strategical purposes. The inhabitants of Kalkilia were
later allowed to return and rebuild their homes.

When the plight of the new refugees started to make
headlines around the world, alienating many of those
who had been sympathetic to Israel during the war itself, the Israeli Government declared that it was prepared to let the new refugees come back. However, this
was a tactical move, designed to blunt criticism; there
never seems to have been any intention to let the bulk
of the refugees return. In the end, less than ten per cent
were allowed to come back, and many of these failed to
return because the permits often did not include whole
families, but only the older people.

Thus the 1967 war has, in a way, aggravated the situation, both by creating a huge number of new refugees and by deepening the conviction in the Arab mind that Israel, whenever possible, will grab new territory and evict its owners. I am deeply convinced that the behavior of the Israeli Government in this situation is altogether shortsighted. As one officer of the Israeli Army put it, "If we already have a million and a quarter Arabs in the areas now controlled by Israel, what difference does it make if we have a hundred thousand more or less? It only alienates the Arabs who stayed behind." This is exactly the point. If the government had been capable of adopting a strategy of peace, it would have behaved differently. For indeed, the new situation created by the war offered Israel chances it never had before.

There are hundreds of thousands of refugees in Israeli-held territory. Some of them, in the Gaza Strip, had been living for twenty years under Egyptian occupation, deprived of all civil rights, living in squalid camps within the Strip, which had become one big concentration camp itself. They could not go to Egypt without a permit, which few got. Perched together in a tiny territory, subsisting on daily rations provided by the United Nations Relief Agency (which also provided them with adequate schools and medical services) they lived a life devoid of hope, in degenerating idleness. The fate of the refugees in the West Bank area, under Jordanian control, was somewhat better. They were considered Jordanian citizens and some of them found work; but, on the whole, they also lived idle lives, subsisting on United Nations relief, often detested by the established inhabitants of the area. Their huge refugee camps were a breeding ground for infiltrators into Israel.

On the morrow of the 1967 war, when these areas were overrun by the Israeli Army, Israel could and should have set in motion a grand operation to settle these refugees. With Israeli know-how—and international capital easily available for this purpose—it could have set up new housing schemes, and new means of production, agricultural and industrial. Starting with some model settlements on the West Bank and reunification of families in Israel itself, such an operation would have captured the imagination of the world and shown how easily these tragic remnants of former wars can become useful human beings again.

A completely new atmosphere could have been created overnight. It would have opened the doors for a reconciliation between Israel and the Palestinian people. It would have prepared the ground for the creation of a Palestinian federation, one of whose first tasks would have been to settle *all* the refugees within the territory of Palestine; the cooperation of Israel and a Palestinian-Arab republic in the solution of the refugee problem would have cemented the federation and given it immediate meaning.

All this would have been popular even in Israel. Many Israelis who have been afraid these many years of the return of all the refugees to the State of Israel, but who were troubled by the existence of the refugee problem, eagerly awaited a resettlement scheme in the West Bank area independent of any decision about the future political fate of the occupied territories.

Why did the Israeli Government miss such an obvious historical opportunity? The answer lies in the incapacity of the present government, composed as it is of many divergent elements, to make up its mind about a positive solution to the questions posed by the 1967 conquests. Those who advocate annexation, of course, would like the territories to be as empty of inhabitants as possible. In the absence of a decision, the traditional traits of Zionism operated, consciously and unconsciously, creating new trouble on top of the old.

13: Pax Semitica

SOME MONTHS before the outbreak of the Six-Day War, I met a high-ranking member of the Egyptian regime. The meeting took place in Paris through the auspices of a mutual friend. Throughout the years, I have met many leaders of the different Arab states, exchanging opinions and trading ideas for a settlement. But this meeting was different.

At the outset, I said to my new-found friend: "Let's make a list of all possible solutions to the Israeli-Arab conflict. Let's analyze every solution in turn and see where we get."

Taking a pen, we wrote the following list on the paper cloth on our table in the Paris restaurant:

(A) Annihilation by war
(B) The destruction of Israel by political and economic isolation
(C) Status quo
(D) A Semitic federation.

*   *   *

The easiest solution of the problem would have been, of course, a decisive military victory by either side. If Israel could achieve a military victory big enough to compel the Arabs to accept an Israeli *diktat*, this would be one answer. But Israel would have to conquer the whole Arab world, an impossible feat even with the unquestioned superiority of the Israeli Army; the brilliant victory in the Six-Day War has now proved that one cannot dictate peace by military means. As General Dayan said four months after the war, "If anyone thought the Arabs had learned a lesson, he was mistaken." If the Arabs could conquer and annihilate Israel, that certainly would be a clear-cut solution. But my Arab partner at the dinner table readily agreed that no such possibility exists. The military superiority of Israel will remain for a long time, and new weapons systems eventually will be introduced in the Middle East which will make it virtually certain that the destruction of Israel will be accompanied by the destruction of the Arab centers of population, thus setting the Region back at least two thousand years (and probably causing a thermonuclear holocaust all over the world). Both of us agreed that we must discount a military solution. (I assume that my partner realized how right he was a few months later, when the Six-Day War proved the point.)

The second proposal is dear to the Arab heart. Drawing an interesting—but, as we have seen, incomplete—analogy with the history of the Crusaders, Arabs tend to delude themselves that Israel can be wished away by not recognizing its existence. An economic and political boycott, they believe, can go on for so long that Israel will eventually wither away.

"We waited two hundred years for the Crusader

State to disappear," Arabs will often say, "and we shall wait another two hundred years for the disappearance of Israel."

I asked my partner quite frankly, "Do you really want to hold up the march of Arab nationalism for two hundred years, just waiting for us to disappear? As long as we are here, and there is no solution to our conflict, you will not get anywhere in the fulfillment of your real aspirations. The conflict opens the Region for foreign intervention, both Western and Soviet, turning us all into pawns of a foreign game. No Arab unity can be achieved as long as a hostile Israel cuts the southern part of the Arab world off from the northern part. And the money you need for industrialization and reform, in order to create a modern and developed Arab society, you now must spend on arms which will become more expensive from year to year.

"Furthermore," I asked, "do you know of one single instance, in modern times, in which a sovereign state has just disappeared because of an economic or political boycott? During the last twenty years, in spite of the boycott, Israel has expanded both politically and economically in many parts of the world." After some discussion, we agreed that no such solution is practical.

Continuing the status quo cannot be considered a solution even in theory. Things will not right themselves automatically. Time is not the great healer in such a situation, with mutual hatred and fear intensifying from generation to generation. Indeed, this attitude is dangerous, taking into account the probable introduction of nuclear weapons into the region in the not-far-distant future. Such introduction seems inevitable. As long as the vicious circle continues to dominate the scene, with Israel fearing attack at any minute, no one can seriously expect the Israeli leadership to abstain for long from producing the ultimate weapon, a feat which Israel could attain, many experts believe, in a matter of months. On the other hand, in the same circumstances, the Arab leadership, fearing Israeli expansion, cannot tolerate a situation in which Israel has the bomb and the Arabs don't. If Israel produces the bomb, one can expect Egypt or Syria, at least, to pay any price, including a part of national independence, to get the bomb from Soviet Russia or China. One must also consider the possibilities inherent in a French-Arab alliance. It was at the height of the French-Israeli alliance that Israel started to develop its nuclear potential. Some people believe that the possession of nuclear bombs by Israel and the Arabs would ensure peace as does the balance of terror between the United States and the Soviet Union. This is an extremely dangerous fallacy. If anything, the 1967 war has proved that in the explosive Middle Eastern situation, a war can break out any time without anyone wanting it. Moreover, in any Middle Eastern state, power may be usurped by a reckless adventurer who, one hopes, could not come to power in Washington or Moscow. The status quo in our Region is a very fragile thing indeed.

We did not write down, on our tablecloth, another theoretical solution, alien to the Arabs but popular in Israel. This is the idea that the great powers would compel the Arabs to make peace—peace meaning, of course, a peace acceptable to the Israelis, obliging the Arabs to recognize the status quo. According to this wishful thinking often voiced by Ben-Gurion and most Israeli leaders, some day Americans and Russians will meet and decide that it is in their mutual interest to impose a peace in our Region. It is just a question of waiting for the two great powers to settle their little differences throughout the world. This is sheer nonsense. Not only is it highly unlikely for the two superpowers to put an end to their rivalry in the Middle East, but even if they did this would only change the character of the Israeli-Arab confrontation without ending it. The Arabs would get from China the weapons they now receive from the Soviet Union—and more dangerous ones.

Throughout the Middle East there persists the naive notion that the conflict was created in some devious way by British imperialism and American intervention, and that we otherwise would all have lived happily ever after. This is a superficial view; as we have seen, the vicious circle was created by the clash of two authentic historical movements. Foreign influences acted on this situation but did not create it. If these influences were removed tomorrow—by some Divine intervention—the confrontation between the two movements would still go on. The solution, then, has to be found between the two sides themselves.

* * *

The first part of the solution I propose is the setting up of a federation between Israel and a new Arab-Palestinian republic, as outlined earlier. This, together with the settlement of the refugees, can be done by Israel in cooperation with the Palestinian Arabs, independent of any official contact between Israel and the Arab states.

The second part of the solution is Semitic Union, a great confederacy of all the states in the Region.

The two parts are not contradictory. I do not view the Palestinian federation as a replacement for a general Israeli-Arab peace. On the contrary, such a peace will be much easier to achieve once the Palestinian problem is solved by common consent. The Palestinian problem is both the reason and the pretext for the belligerent attitude of the other Arab nations toward Israel. In all their statements, Arab leaders maintain that the only reason for their war against Israel is either to "liberate Palestine" or to "restore the rights of the Palestinian-Arab people." Once the Arabs of Palestine declare themselves liberated and agree that their rights have been restored, the main obstacle to peace will have been removed. Or, to put it another way, those Arab leaders who wish, deep in their hearts, to reach some settlement with Israel will be able to say so and act accordingly once the Palestinian problem has been solved. Before this, any such statement or action would be considered treason against the Palestinian Arabs. Thus, a solution in Palestine is almost a prerequisite to a general Semitic peace settlement, and at the same time, a Semitic peace is necessary to make the Palestinian solution meaningful and enduring.

I would like to explain here why I use the term *Semitic*. The reason has nothing to do with race; indeed, in the Middle East race is as uncertain as anywhere in the world. Both to Hebrews and to Arabs, race, today, means little. The term *Semitic* should, rather, be viewed as emphasizing an historical heritage, common to all peoples speaking languages of the Semitic family—Arabic, Hebrew, Amharic, and so forth. It also emphasizes the common cultural and spiritual background of all the peoples of our Region, so much influenced by their past. In this respect, the Semitic family of culture includes even the Turks, the Kurds, and the Persians, who are descended from different races and speak non-

Semitic languages, but whose history is bound up with
the culture of the Semitic world and the great religions
of the Semites. Yet the main reason for the indispensa-
bility of this term is that it automatically includes
Arabs and Hebrews, explains itself readily in the Region and throughout the world, and has the same meaning in all languages.

It is my deepest belief—and perhaps the point at
which my friends and I differ from other people who
aspire to peace in the Region—that such a peace cannot and must not contradict the national aspirations of
both Hebrews and Arabs. Nationalism will reign supreme in our generation in all the countries of the Region, and nothing will stop it. Any idea, inspiring as it
may be, which runs counter to the national feelings of
the people concerned, will be by-passed by history.

I am a Hebrew nationalist, and I want to deal with
Arab nationalists. I want to tell them: The last fifty
years have shown that neither you nor we can achieve
our national aspirations as long as we fight each other.
Our two great national movements can neutralize each
other, or they can be combined in one great regional
movement of liberation and progress. This is what the
Semitic idea means—an ideal combining the two nationalisms, an ideal with which nationalists on both
sides can identify.

* * *

Joining a great Semitic confederacy would mean, for
Israel, putting an end to the Zionist chapter in its history and starting a new one—the chapter of Israel as a
state integrated in its Region, playing a part in the Region's struggle for progress and unity.

For the Arabs it would mean recognition of a post-Zionist Israel as a part of the Region, a part which could and should not be abolished because, in its new form, it is a factor in the struggle for the common good.

Let me be quite clear about this. A lot of nonsense has been written about solutions which do not recognize the existence of Israel as a sovereign state. Not one single Israeli, and certainly not I, would ever agree to any such solution. The existence of Israel as a sovereign state is the point of departure for any solution, as much as the rights and the aspirations of the Palestinian nation and any other Arab people.

Semitic Union not only provides a framework for mutual acceptance, but has many other advantages.

• First, it would end mutual fear and suspicion, the most dangerous elements in the present situation. Providing for common defense and coordinating the military affairs of all member states, it would make possible a gradual general disarmament and de-nuclearization with mutual inspection. By abolishing military secrecy, it would safeguard everyone from surprise attacks and surprise concentrations of troops—such as the Egyptian one which triggered the 1967 war, or the imaginary Israeli one on the Syrian front which led up to it.

• Union would also mean a pooling of political power. Joining the Union, Israel would, at long last, align itself with the prevalent trend in the Afro-Asian world and support those Arab struggles for liberation which are still unresolved. Israel's influence in the world would be put at the disposal of a Regional leadership, giving such leadership an impact which it lacked even at the height of Abd-el-Nasser's successes as a leader of the "Third World."

• Economically, the potential advantages are enormous. For Israel, it would mean the end of Arab boycotts and the integration of its economy into the Region. For the Arabs it would mean the possibility of meaningful Regional planning, a Semitic common market which would harness the immense wealth of Arab oil to the cause of progress and industrialization of the Arab peoples, especially Egypt.

• A united Region, liberated from fear and foreign exploitation, could start at long last a rapid march toward the modernization of the whole Region, restoring it to the place it held both in ancient and Islamic times.

• It would mean breaking the vicious circle, which has embittered the lives of too many for too long, and starting a new cycle of mutual fertilization—a peaceful competition for the common good instead of a military competition, which can only end in mutual disaster.

* * *

All this sounds very optimistic. Indeed, it is.

I am an optimist. I believe that nothing in history is pre-determined. History in the making is composed of acts of human beings, their emotions and aspirations.

The depth of bitterness and hatred throughout our Semitic Region seems bottomless. Yet it is a comparatively new phenomenon, the outcome of the recent clash of our peoples. Nothing like European anti-Semitism ever existed in the Arab world prior to the events which created the vicious circle.

We have seen, in our times, Germans and Frenchmen cooperating, if not loving each other, after a war which lasted for many hundreds of years and whose bitter fruits are deeply embedded in both German and French culture. We are witnessing today the beginnings of an American-Soviet alliance which would have been unthinkable only a dozen years ago.

We are not dealing, therefore, with mystical phenomena, but with matters which can be changed by policy decisions, by new ideas, new leaders and new political forces—in short, by a new generation all over the Middle East disgusted with the mess their fathers have made and by the conventional lies of propaganda.

The first step has to be made by Israel. Throughout the last three generations, since the appearance of the first Zionist settlers in Palestine, it has been our side which has held the initiative, the Arabs reacting to our actions. It is up to us to change, by deliberate steps, the climate of hatred and suspicion in the Middle East.

We can start this by helping the Palestinian Arabs to set up their state and by settling the refugees. We can assume a completely new stance in the Region by supporting Arab nationalist aims in spirit and action, with a hundred small gestures, each insignificant by itself but contributing, in sum, to a gradual change in the atmosphere. By truly integrating the Israeli Arabs into the framework of our state and turning it into a pluralistic society, we can show the Arab world a new face—Israeli Arabs representing Israel, side by side with Hebrew Israelis, in all fields of endeavor, from the General Assembly of the United Nations to the playground of international soccer.

Nothing will change overnight. Each of our acts will be suspect in the beginning. Each will be denounced as a new Zionist plot. But slowly, by concerted action, suspicion will be dispelled and confidence gained, pro-

viding the psychological framework for new Arab policies.

*   *   *

Yet time is important.

An uneasy cease-fire prevails along the frozen fronts
of the recent war, a cease-fire fraught with dangers,
broken by intermittent shots.

The armies confronting each other across the cease-
fire lines are arming quickly. A new war is assumed by
all of them as a virtual certainty, with only the exact
timing still in doubt. But the next war, or the one after
it, will be quite different from the recent one, so different, in fact, that the *blitzkrieg* of June 1967, will look,
in comparison, like a humanitarian exercise.

Nuclear weapons, missiles of all types, are nearing
the Semitic scene. Their advent is inevitable. If the
vicious circle is not broken, and broken soon, it will
lead, with the preordained certainty of a Greek tragedy,
toward a holocaust that will bury Tel Aviv and Cairo,
Damascus and Jerusalem.

Semitic suicide is the only alternative to Semitic
peace.

A different kind of tragedy is brewing in Palestine
itself. If no just solution is found soon, the guerrilla war
of organizations like *al-Fatah* will start a vicious circle
of its own, a steep spiral of terror and counter-terror,
killing and retaliation, sabotage and mass deportation,
which will bring undreamt of miseries to the Palestinian
people. It will poison the atmosphere and generate a
nightmare that will make peace impossible in our lifetime, turning Israel into an armed and beleaguered
camp forever, bringing the Arab march toward progress
to a complete standstill, and perhaps spelling the end of

the Palestinian-Arab people as a nation—the very people for whose freedom *al-Fatah* fights in vain.

Cease fire—this is not a passive imperative. In order to cease fire, acts of peace must be done. Peace must be waged—actively, imaginatively, incessantly. In the words of the psalmist: "Seek peace and pursue it." The search can be passive—the pursuit cannot.

*   *   *

One of the most beautiful books of the Bible, *Ecclesiastes*, contains a passage which has often disturbed me: "A time to kill, and a time to heal."

Did the Preacher really mean that there is a time to kill? Did he mean to advocate killing at any time?

I don't think so. I see the Preacher as a man full of wisdom and experience, who knew all human follies. He knew that, people being what they are, there are times when war cannot be averted. He wanted to say that after such a war, people must set about to build peace, to wage peace as they have waged war.

In these pages I have passed harsh judgment on both Zionists and Arabs, about their foolishness and short-sightedness. In theory, they could have acted differently, and thereby avoided untold suffering. But movements like theirs are children of their age, victims of its illusions and limitations; thus, Zionist and Arab could not really have behaved differently. Understanding this, we of a later time must set a new course.

It is thus that I understand the words of *Ecclesiastes*:

A time to be born, and a time to die;

A time to plant, and a time to pluck up what is planted;

A time to kill, and a time to heal;

A time to break down, and a time to build up;

A time to weep, and a time to laugh;

A time to mourn, and a time to dance;

A time to cast away stones, and a time to gather stones together;

A time to embrace, and a time to refrain from embracing;

A time to seek, and a time to lose;

A time to keep, and a time to cast away;

A time to rend, and a time to sew;

A time to keep silence, and a time to speak;

A time to love, and a time to hate;

A time for war, and a time for peace.

This chapter of *Ecclesiastes* starts with the sentence: "For everything there is a season, and a time for every matter under heaven."

The time for peace is now.

Epilogue

14: Four Years Later

"The time for peace is now." It was with these words that I concluded the writing of this book four years ago.

They have been four years of dramatic events, during which peace sometimes seemed to lurk just around the corner, but at other times seemed to be billions of light-years away.

During these four years, we have witnessed the rise and decline of the *Fedayeen* movement; the bombing of the Egyptian heartland and the beginning of Soviet involvement; the War of Attrition and the cease-fire; and the Rogers plan and the Jarring mission. Nasser and Eshkol have died, Sadat and Golda Meir have become world figures. For the first time, Egypt has declared its readiness to make peace with Israel. And for the first time, Israel has declared, through the pronouncements of Moshe Dayan, that it prefers the annexation of certain areas rather than peace.

Everything seems to have changed, yet nothing has. Were the Preacher of *Ecclesiastes* to come around

again in the guise of a duly accredited foreign correspondent, he would find nothing to add to his former
dispatch: "The thing that hath been, it is that which
shall be, and that which is done is that which shall be
done, and there is no new thing under the sun. Is there
anything whereof it may be said, See, this is new?"

*   *   *

In this book, I have tried to describe how The War
Nobody Wanted came about. I have shown how the
leaders of nations—some of them wise, all of them
clever—imagined that they were controlling events,
while all the time they were actually being controlled by
the mechanism of the Vicious Circle, something they
were unable to understand.

It is this mechanism, created by events which took
place in our Region three generations ago, that continues to make real change nearly impossible. New
powers, new personalities, new weapons—all are drawn
into this Vicious Circle like so many twigs into a whirl-
pool.

The utter helplessness of Israeli and Arab leaders in
dealing with the effects of this historical mechanism
may be predictable, because the leaders themselves are
in reality the creations of the processes which they seem
to be creating. But it is the helplessness of a Nixon and
a Kosygin that must amaze and frighten the world. For
despite their self-confidence about negotiating the troubled waters of international diplomacy, they too have
been relentlessly sucked into the Middle Eastern whirl-
pool.

A civilization born in Jerusalem may be destroyed
and an entire world may go to pieces just because of

Jerusalem—if the Vicious Circle controlling our lives in this region is not broken.

We must be able to discern this dangerous mechanism, to understand it. We must learn to control it. Otherwise, it may destroy us.

* * *

Modern medicine has made possible the transplantation of the heart of one human being into the living body of another. But it has not yet found a way to make the body accept the transplant permanently.

The body does not want the transplant. So it tries with all its might to evict the newcomer. This is seemingly a command of nature, probably going back millions of years to the beginning of organic life.

Even if the body knew that it was given the heart to keep itself alive, it would still shout: Go away; you are foreign; I don't want you!

If the new heart could reply, it would shout back: Body, I've come to save you; if you reject me, we'll both die; without me, you are condemned!

It would be a hopeless dialogue.

The story of Zionism in the Middle East is something like this. Israel is a giant transplant.

No analogy can be considered entirely valid, but I do find this one helpful.

The early Zionist settlers were convinced that they were saving not only themselves and their people, but also the Arab peoples around them. They were perplexed, astounded, and progressively angered when the Arab world rejected them instinctively, as though obeying a biological command.

Today, the Arab body continues to reject the re-territorialized Israeli nation planted in its midst. Israel, fighting back and winning, has by now nearly forgotten that all it was fighting for initially was acceptance by the body.

The Arabs see Israel not only as an unwanted transplant but as a spreading malignancy that threatens their very existence. The Israelis see the Arabs surrounding them as an eternal menace, eternally rejecting them: "The Arabs will never make peace."

These two conceptions, reinforced by the experience of three generations and maintaining themselves automatically, perpetuate the Vicious Circle. They act like all mental patterns by absorbing and intensifying every scrap of information that reinforces them, by ignoring and rejecting every fact—small, big, or even stupendous—which runs counter to them.

The events of the last four years—the seventh day of the Six-Day War—demonstrate this over and over again.

* * *

The salient fact of these years is that neither side has spoken to the other.

They have shot at each other, bombarded and bombed each other, even taunted each other across the 200 yards of the Suez Canal. But never, never has either of them said a single word to the other.

This is stranger than it seems at first sight.

Gamal Abd-el-Nasser did accept the U.N. Security Council resolution 242 of November 1967—the resolution that in effect proposed withdrawal of Israeli forces, more or less to the old frontiers, in return for mutual acceptance, official recognition, and lasting peace. Following that, Nasser offered peace through foreign correspondents. Since then, Anwar Sadat, his less glamorous and therefore more practical heir, has offered peace through the U.S. State Department. Yet not once has Sadat talked to the Israelis themselves. Not once has he addressed a simple, forthright speech to the Israeli people, saying to them: We are at war; we want peace; get out of our territory and, whether we like you or not, we will try to live with you.

Similarly, while shouting to the whole world that it now wants peace with Israel, Egypt has not done the simplest thing on earth: invite the leaders of the Israeli peace movement to Cairo and talk with them openly for all the world to see and hear. Such an act would demonstrate dramatically and unequivocally to every Israeli that more than diplomatic tactics have changed.

Israel, on the other hand, has said scores of times that all it seeks is peace, real peace, nothing but peace. But when Sadat offered peace, not clandestinely, but speaking openly to the world and to his own people, the government of Israel reacted as though once again it had been stabbed in the back by the treacherous Arabs—indeed, as though Sadat's peace thrust had been the unkindest cut of all.

In all its maneuvers, including innumerable calls for "direct talks," the Israeli government has not once really addressed itself to the Arab world, saying simply: We don't want your territory; all we want are peace and security; convince us that you really mean it and we'll gladly go back to the old borders; we'll even try to make amends to the Palestinians.

Neither side can talk to the other, because neither side sees the other as the other really is. And because of this, everything done in the Middle East still achieves the opposite of its conscious intention—when it achieves anything at all.

*   *   *

Consider the story of Soviet involvement and how it came about.

Immediately after the Six-Day War, Egypt was the principal architect of the so-called Khartoum resolution, which proved to be a catastrophe of major proportions for the Arab world and a present for Israeli annexationists. By proclaiming the three "No's"—No negotiations, No recognition, No peace treaty—the Arab world reinforced the determination of Israel to stay where it was, deep in Arab territory and poised for war. As it was, very few Israelis needed such reinforcement.

When it became obvious that Israeli occupation had become a permanent fact, Abd-el-Nasser started the War of Attrition in order to revive the issue and deny any hint of permanence to the occupation. Conditioned by his mental image of the enemy, he threatened Israel with seas of blood and horizons aflame if it refused to implement the U.N. Security Council's resolution. And conditioned by their own mental image of the Arabs, the Israel leaders blocked out Nasser's "if" and let only his threat come through, loud and clear.

Meanwhile, people were dying along the Suez Canal. Mothers in Israel listened to the hourly newscasts, expecting to hear that another Israeli soldier had been killed—a soldier who could be theirs.

In order to end the strain, the Israeli government started the bombing of Egypt in depth. In spite of later denials, the government's aim was undoubtedly to bomb the Nasser regime into submission. And undoubtedly this aim received some active American encouragement. But anyone who was not blinded by abysmal contempt for the Arab world could and did foresee that the Arabs would react like any other people similarly attacked: They rallied around their leaders. This bombing in depth reinforced Abd-el-Nasser, just as the Khartoum resolution reinforced the war-coalition in Israel.

Golda Meir later asserted, in an official interview, that when the fateful decision to bomb Egypt's heartland was taken, not one of the ministers in her cabinet warned her that it might lead to Soviet intervention. Yet it must have been—and indeed was—clear to any thoughtful observer that, after the Soviet Union's colossal political, economic, and military investment in Egypt, any real threat to Cairo would provoke a massive Soviet response.

With the arrival in Egypt of Soviet missile personnel, combat pilots, and "advisers"—an event ominously reminiscent of the United States's Viet Nam blunder, an event without Soviet precedent outside the Communist bloc—Middle Eastern realities changed radically. The Vicious Circle did not cease to operate. But its inherent dangers multiplied tremendously.

* * *

The Rogers plan, leading to a reactivation of the Jarring mission, was a direct outcome of the new Soviet involvement.

The plan was based on two interrelated fears: that a new conflagration between the Semitic peoples would probably lead to the total destruction of all U.S. interests in the Arab world, with incalculable consequences to the Western world; and that such a conflict could quickly get out of hand and bring about a world war—as had the shooting of an Austrian duke at Sarajevo in 1914.

The Rogers plan is intelligent, practical, and even-handed. It has all the merits of a sober solution advanced by outsiders unaffected by the emotions of the belligerents. It has only one drawback: It lies well beyond the psychologically acceptable world of the belligerents—two peoples who cannot look at each other without seeing horrible monsters.

You don't give back conquered territory to a monster who will inevitably spring at your throat the next minute. You don't start talking with a monster who has conquered your territory and who will inevitably grab more at the first opportunity.

For a long time, I was the only member of the Israeli Parliament who openly supported the Rogers plan—as a result of which I was called many names, some of them quite unparliamentary. I have talked to some of the plan's authors and been favorably impressed. I am even ready to confess that I prefer an imposed peace to a voluntary war.

But I do not believe that the efforts of foreign diplomats from outside the Region, addressing themselves to governments, can bring about peace. Peace must come from within, from a change of mind on both sides. Even a temporary settlement, a "small peace," cannot occur without a massive mobilization of the forces of peace on both sides. If these diplomats can normally do very little, they seem to do even less in encouraging and aiding these authentic forces of peace. And yet without these forces, the manifold efforts of a Sisco, a Jarring, or a Kosygin are no more than the labors of Sisyphus.

* * *

Is a change of mind on both sides possible?

Contrary to the Preacher in *Ecclesiastes*, I do believe that there are things whereof it may be said: See, this is new!

For an Egyptian president to speak openly about the possibility of peace with Israel, a psychological revolution of great magnitude was needed. Many Egyptians, like many other Arabs, are sick and tired of what has become the Endless War. There is a mood evident in Egypt—perhaps only for a fleeting moment—to see if some kind of peace can be obtained without giving up Arab land, without sacrificing the Palestinian refugees.

This mood has led to an Egyptian dialogue with the United States rather than with Israel. The old mental image of Israel as being nothing more than a U.S. puppet, a creation of Western imperialism, still deludes Arabs into believing that an arrangement with the United States will solve the Israeli problem.

But it won't.

In Israel, the abortive Goldmann mission—a hinted Egyptian invitation to an old, half-Israeli Zionist that was torpedoed by Golda Meir—was enough to trigger an outburst of popular indignation, which indicated the depth of the peace sentiment among Israelis. This public response created a mood that, coupled with the Soviet threat and U.S. pressure, induced the Golda Meir cabinet to enter the new Jarring talks. It also broke up the war-coalition, thereby leaving the most rabid annexationists outside the government.

This national mood was neither strong enough nor lasting enough to compel the Israeli government to agree to the acceptance of the Rogers formula of withdrawal to the old frontiers "with insubstantial alterations" in return for formal peace. In fact, many leading Israelis have said openly that they would prefer another war to giving up some territory or other—Sharem-el-Sheikh, the Golan heights, the Gaza Strip, the Jordan valley, depending on the personal preferences of the speaker. They believe that if only the Arabs are hit on the head once more, they will surely be ready for peace on Israel's terms.

The Arabs won't be.

Nevertheless, the moods of 1971 are significantly different from the moods of 1967. They indicate that national moods can change, even if they have not yet changed enough to break down the established mental patterns that perpetuate the Vicious Circle.

* * *

The most crucial part of the change concerns the Israeli-Palestinian relationship.

The rebirth of the Palestinian phoenix, so similar to the rebirth of the Hebrew nation, has been by far the most significant fact of the post-1967 era. The rise of the *Fedayeen* movement ranks as one of its major manifestations.

The movement has succeeded in demonstrating to the world that a Palestinian nation does indeed exist and that it cannot be ignored with impunity. The movement evoked sympathy in many international circles, and has even become romanticized in some parts of the New Left.

However, after four years, the *Fedayeen* have not

succeeded in winning over the most Palestinian of all Palestinians—the population of the Israeli-occupied West Bank, the heart of Palestine. There, guerrilla warfare has practically died out. In Gaza, though, it has been kept alive by misery and despair among the Arabs and by a declared Israeli policy of annexation.

On the East Bank, old Transjordan, the *Fedayeen* lost the terrible civil wars—more exactly, the massacres —of 1970 and 1971. The masses of Palestinians living there have not risen against King Hussein's Bedouin army. Consequently, the *Fedayeen* have been left to fight the hopeless battle alone.

Why?

Every Palestinian identifies himself, in some way, with the *Fedayeen*—the only independent fighting forces of his people. The *Fedayeen* have given back to the Palestinians their national dignity, their feeling of national identity. They have done for the Palestinians what Zionism has done for the Jews.

But most Palestinians realize that the official *Fedayeen* program is about as realistic as a plan to give North America back to the Indians. Such a program could be achieved only by a victorious war—and every Palestinian from Jerusalem and Nablus knows perfectly well what that means.

West Bankers want to end the Israeli military occupation—not that the occupation is a particularly harsh one, but rather because, as an Arab friend of mine remarked, "If I have a splinter in my eye, I don't care whether it is of iron or gold." Palestinians in general want a solution: They want freedom and an end to the misery of the refugees. But they are not in the mood to wait for four generations. When Arafat promises to fight the Zionists as Muslims once fought the Crusaders, no Arab is likely to forget that the Kingdom of Jerusalem lasted for a hundred years and the Kingdom of Acre for another hundred.

The *Fedayeen* program may make sense in San Francisco and Rome. It does not in Tulkarm and Amman.

It is the old story all over again: While trying to start a war of liberation, the *Fedayeen* leaders have been quite incapable, so far, of liberating themselves from the old mental patterns. Demanding recognition for their own dispersed nation, they have been unable to bring themselves to extend recognition to the Israeli nation. Few wars are won by ignoring your enemy; this one is no exception.

Much as the Egyptians offered peace to the Americans, the *Fedayeen* have been offering peace to the New Left of Paris, London, and New York. They talk about the creation of a "Democratic, Non-Sectarian Palestine," where "Jews, Muslims, and Christians" will live peacefully together in equality and justice. But they most emphatically refuse to meet and talk with any of these "Jews" with whom they want to live.

There are, in Palestine, no "Jews, Muslims, and Christians." That is, there is no conflict among religions, for religion is a marginal, if not irrelevant, factor. Rather, there is a conflict between nations—the Jewish-Israeli and Arab-Palestinian nations. Mutual recognition is a prerequisite to peace. It can lead to the coexistence of two national states and eventually, I hope, to confederacy and federation.

*   *   *

Today, there is a growing awareness of this possibility within the Palestinian camp. And perhaps this book, as originally published in 1968, has had something to do with it. *Fedayeen* leaders, accusing each other of secretly favoring the creation of a Palestinian state alongside Israel instead of on the ruins of Israel, frequently refer to this solution as "the Avnery Plan."

This compliment is quite undeserved. No one, and certainly no Israeli, is the author of an idea so natural, so self-evident, as the acceptance of the facts of life in our Region. These facts suggest the existence of two nations, both with an inherent right to self-determination, independence, and security, one being Israel, the other being a new, sovereign state of Palestine.

Four years ago everybody was against this solution. King Hussein was not inclined to give up the territory annexed by his grandfather and content himself with the kingdom initially carved out of the desert for his family by Winston Churchill, exactly 50 years ago. The *Fedayeen* rejected this solution, thereby compelling all pro-*Fedayeen* Arab governments to follow suit. The United States was against a solution that would weaken, as it thought, its client regimes in the Arab world. The Soviet Union, uncharacteristically monarchical, supported the royal ally of Egypt. And the Israeli governments of Levi Eshkol and Golda Meir were dead set against any mention of a Palestinian people—a skeleton kept in a tightly shut closet.

Now, four years later, much has changed. President Nixon has declared, in his foreign policy report to Congress of February 25, 1971, that "No lasting peace can be achieved in the Middle East without addressing the legitimate aspirations of the Palestinian people." Nine days earlier, Assistant Secretary of State Joseph Sisco had assured his audience on a "Face the Nation" television broadcast that "Even in the *Fedayeen* movement itself there are some very modest signs . . . that at least some Palestinians are thinking about the notion of a political solution based on the idea of coexistence with Israel."

King Hussein has offered his Palestinian subjects self-determination and the option to create an autonomous Palestinian state after liberation—"after" being the operational word. Few believe this promise, but the very fact that it was considered necessary to make it at all is a sign of the times.

Egypt, the Soviet Union, and others have been variously reported as considering and even embracing the two-state solution. This leaves only the Israeli government, alone in the whole wide world, adamantly opposed to the idea of an independent Palestinian state in the Arab parts of Palestine, areas that are today under Israeli military occupation. But even in Israel things are moving.

Not so long ago, Golda Meir was still saying: "It was not as though there was a Palestine people in Palestine . . . and we came and threw them out and took their country away from them. They did not exist." And on another occasion: "There is no Palestinian people. There never was one."

But nowadays, after public opinion polls have shown that the majority of young Israelis favor recognition of the Palestinian people, even Golda has changed her tune if not her music. She still insists that there is room only for "two states between the Mediterranean and Iraq." One is Israel; the other may be called Jordan or Palestine, for all she cares. This is progress of sorts, coming from a lady who until recently apparently did not know that Palestinians even existed.

* * *

Where is all of this leading us?

Prophecy is a notoriously dangerous profession in my land, for it can end on the cross, in pits of mire, in fiery furnaces. So I have no ambition at all to follow such a course.

Writing on the eve of Israel's 23rd Day of Independence, which is also the 1441st day of the Six-Day War, I believe another war is quite possible and may well be already a part of the past when this epilogue appears in print. Outside pressure for an imposed peace settlement —before, after, or instead of such a war—may become strong enough to make a diplomatic breakthrough possible. Everything is fluid, many things are possible.

Political circumstances change. So do military facts. So do international alignments. But the most difficult and most important of all changes is the one that affects the minds of men and nations. It is my hope that this book may play a small part in helping to bring about this vital change.

Everyone talks of liberation in our Region, but the only liberation of lasting value is the liberation from yesterday's images, from the prison of our own mental patterns.

Everyone proclaims revolution in our Region. But there is nothing in the Middle East as revolutionary as peace.

Today, as it was four years ago, the time for peace is NOW.

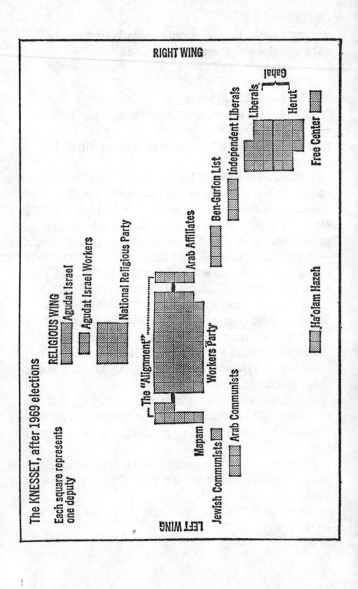

The KNESSET, after 1969 elections

Each square represents one deputy

RIGHT WING

RELIGIOUS WING

Agudat Israel

Agudat Israel Workers

National Religious Party

Gahal

Liberals

Independent Liberals

Herut

Ben-Gurion List

Free Center

Arab Affiliates

The "Alignment"

Workers Party

Mapam

Jewish Communists

Arab Communists

Ha'olam Hazeh

LEFT WING

Index

Index